Robert C. Salisbury

Correspondence of King James VI. of Scotland with Sir Robert Cecil and Others in England,

during the reign of Queen Elizabeth; with an appendix containing papers illustrative of transactions between King James and Robert Earl of Essex.

Robert C. Salisbury

Correspondence of King James VI. of Scotland with Sir Robert Cecil and Others in England, *during the reign of Queen Elizabeth; with an appendix containing papers illustrative of transactions between King James and Robert Earl of Essex.*

ISBN/EAN: 9783337324131

Printed in Europe, USA, Canada, Australia, Japan

Cover: Foto ©ninafisch / pixelio.de

More available books at **www.hansebooks.com**

CORRESPONDENCE
OF
KING JAMES VI. OF SCOTLAND
WITH
SIR ROBERT CECIL AND OTHERS IN ENGLAND,
DURING THE
REIGN OF QUEEN ELIZABETH;
WITH AN APPENDIX
CONTAINING PAPERS ILLUSTRATIVE OF TRANSACTIONS BETWEEN
KING JAMES AND ROBERT EARL OF ESSEX.

PRINCIPALLY PUBLISHED FOR THE FIRST TIME FROM
MANUSCRIPTS OF THE MOST HON. THE MARQUIS OF SALISBURY, K.G.
PRESERVED AT HATFIELD.

EDITED BY JOHN BRUCE, ESQ. F.S.A.

PRINTED FOR THE CAMDEN SOCIETY.

M.DCCC.LXI.

COUNCIL OF THE CAMDEN SOCIETY

FOR THE YEAR 1860-61.

President,
THE MOST HON. THE MARQUESS OF BRISTOL, V.P.S.A.
WILLIAM HENRY BLAAUW, ESQ. M.A., F.S.A.
BERIAH BOTFIELD, ESQ. M.P. F.S.A.
JOHN BRUCE, ESQ. F.S.A. *Director.*
JOHN PAYNE COLLIER, ESQ. F.S.A. *Treasurer.*
WILLIAM DURRANT COOPER, ESQ. F.S.A.
JAMES CROSBY, ESQ. F.S.A.
JOHN FORSTER, ESQ. LL.D.
EDWARD FOSS, ESQ. F.S.A.
THOMAS W. KING, ESQ. F.S.A.
THE REV. LAMBERT B. LARKING, M.A.
JAMES HEYWOOD MARKLAND, ESQ. D.C.L. F.R.S. F.S.A.
FREDERIC OUVRY, ESQ. Treas. S.A.
ROBERT PORRETT, ESQ. F.S.A.
WILLIAM JOHN THOMS, ESQ. F.S.A. *Secretary.*
WILLIAM TITE, ESQ. M.P. F.R.S. F.S.A.

The Council of the Camden Society desire it to be understood that they are not answerable for any opinions or observations that may appear in the Society's publications; the Editors of the several works being alone responsible for the same.

INTRODUCTION.

THERE were circumstances in the condition of England at the close of the sixteenth century which are without a parallel in the history of any other country. The strong hand which had swayed "the rod of empire" for more than forty years, had now grown feeble. The stately and attractive person, by the princely carriage of which Queen Elizabeth had in early life excited the admiration of all beholders, and had raised the attachment of her people to enthusiasm, now bowed and tottered. The flattery of artists and the contrivances of ingenuity were no longer successful. Time's victory was apparent. The tallest of ruffs could not conceal it, the most glittering of diamonds could not overpower it; voice, action, attitude, disclosed it; and the exertions necessary for the performance of the more public duties of her royal function pressed home upon her own consciousness the fact, which politeness forbade her courtiers to disclose. When she met her parliament in 1601, the mere weight of the royal purple overwhelmed her. She staggered, and would have fallen at the foot of the throne—that throne which she had contributed to make one of the noblest in the world—but strong arms were ready, as they always had been, to support her; the brave spirit which dwelt within her put forth its energy; she recovered herself, with a little assistance, and for the last time seated herself in her accustomed chair.

A multitude of similar indications had, for some time before the occurrence just alluded to, convinced every one, that what, up to that moment, had been the greatest reign in our annals, was coming to a close. The thought naturally presented itself—What was to follow? Who was to be the successor? The question was the most important that could be raised. It involved not merely the inquiry as to what individual person should occupy the vacant throne, momentous as that consideration was when the regal authority had been "strained," by Tudor energy, "to a higher pitch than at any previous period"[a] of our history; the inquiry comprehended also the far more weighty question of whether England should still maintain the position among nations to which she had been exalted during the reign of Elizabeth, or whether, entering once more, under a Roman Catholic successor, into the great confederacy of papal Europe, she should abandon Holland to the tender mercies of Spain, and the Huguenots to the dominancy of the party of St. Bartholomew, should renounce her friendship with the German Protestants, should close the sacred oracles which had been to her the source of light and truth, should replace her defaced altars, restore her broken images, banish from her literature the noble works which during the Elizabethan period had been the results and were the evidences of increasing freedom of thought, and should submit the general mind to the fetters of that spiritual authority which had traduced and anathematised Elizabeth and all her doings, and, during the reign of her predecessor, had burnt its true character indelibly into the history of the country.

Judged upon the principles of lawyers and canonists, the question of the succession was one of considerable complication and difficulty.

By a statute passed in the 25th Henry VIII. cap. 22, shortly after the marriage with Ann Boleyn and the birth of Elizabeth, the crown was settled upon the King and his issue male. In default of such issue it was to go to his daughter Elizabeth, passing over Mary as

[a] Forster's Grand Remonstrance, p. 91, ed. 1860.

illegitimate; and if Elizabeth died without issue it was to descend in its accustomed course to the right heirs of Henry VIII. for ever.

By another statute of the same sovereign, passed shortly after the marriage with Jane Seymour (28 Henry VIII. cap. 7), the marriage with Anne Boleyn was declared void, and the succession was limited to the King's sons and their issue, and, in default of sons, to the King's legitimate daughters, which excluded both Mary and Elizabeth. Power was given to the King by this statute, in default of lawful heirs of his body, to direct the succession by letters patent, or by his " last will, made in writing and signed with his most gracious hand."

By a third statute passed seven years afterwards (35 Hen. VIII. cap. 1), immediately before the expedition to Boulogne, after declaring the succession to be in Prince Edward, the heir apparent, it was enacted, that if the Prince should die without issue, the crown should go in succession to the King's daughters Mary and Elizabeth, subject to such conditions as should be limited by the King by letters patent, or by " his last will in writing, signed with his most gracious hand." If no conditions were limited by Henry VIII., then the estates of Mary and Elizabeth were to be absolute; and by another section the King was empowered to direct, by letters patent, or by his last will, what should be the course of the succession in case of want of issue of his children Edward, Mary and Elizabeth."[a]

In pursuance of this power, Henry VIII. made his will on the 30th December, 1546, by which, in default of issue of Edward VI., Mary and Elizabeth, the crown was settled, (I.) on the issue of Lady

---

[a] I am the more particular in stating these provisions, because the power given to the King by this Act of Parliament, of limiting the ultimate succession to the crown in default of issue of his children, has been unaccountably overlooked by Blackstone (Comm. lib. i. cap. 3.), and, so far as I have observed, by all his editors, and by the many writers who have depended upon his accuracy.

Frances, the King's niece, eldest daughter of his late sister Mary, Queen of France, and afterwards Duchess of Suffolk; (II.) on the issue of the Lady Eleanor, the second daughter of the same Mary Duchess of Suffolk: and (III.) on the next rightful heirs.

Under these formal instruments, it could not be doubted that the legal right to the succession to the crown was in the representative of the Lady Frances, the eldest daughter of the House of Suffolk. At certain periods that right had already been strongly affirmed. Sir Nicholas Bacon, when Lord Keeper, was one of its supporters, and during the life of Mary Queen of Scots, the fear of a Roman Catholic successor had multiplied the friends of the House of Suffolk.

But a question was raised in reference to the proper execution of the will of Henry VIII. At the close of his life he used a stamp for the impression of a fac-simile of his signature upon formal documents. It was asserted that this stamp had been employed in the execution of his will, notwithstanding the statute which gave him the power, distinctly prescribed, that it should be executed only by a will "signed with his most gracious hand." One would have thought that this was a question which might have been easily set at rest. But the will was not forthcoming. For a long time it was either mislaid or, more probably, concealed. It is now in the Public Record Office, accessible to all; and no one who has seen it will contend that the king's signature was affixed otherwise than with a pen. In its absence, some persons argued that, even if executed with the King's ordinary stamp, it was a valid document; but that, we suppose, is not an opinion that would be satisfactory to lawyers.

Supposing that King Henry's will were not duly executed, who then would have the right? Unquestionably King James VI. of Scotland, as the representative of Margaret Queen of Scotland, the eldest daughter of Henry VII. Henry VIII. had, in his will, passed over the line of Scotland without notice. He had given the crown, as we have seen, in the case now about to happen, to the line of Suffolk. But that line had no present right except under his will. If that were got rid of, their pretensions were entirely gone, and the crown would legally descend, in default of heirs of the body of Henry VIII. to the nearest representative of the eldest daughter of Henry VII. That person was undoubtedly James of Scotland.

But here arose a new question. James was an alien. Ought he, who, in the language of lawyers, was devoid of inheritable blood, who could not legally succeed to so much as a cottage in England, or an acre of land,—ought he, by right of inheritance, to take the throne? Every mere lawyer thought it "a question not to be asked." Or, again, judging upon wider principles, was it consistent with true policy, or with patriotism, that a foreigner should rule in England? Above all foreigners, should this pre-eminence be given to a Scot, one of a nation whom Englishmen were taught from childhood to despise? Many a brave heart was ready to declare that it was "foul scorn" that it should be so.

Supposing that on such principles King James were rejected, who would come next? The Lady Arabella Stewart, descended from Margaret daughter of Henry VII. in the same manner as King James, save that her father was a second son, and King James's father was the eldest. But she had the fact of her birth and domiciliation within the kingdom of England as a counterpoise to her father's want of primogeniture.

Against Arabella there were raised objections which had weight according to the prepossessions of the considerers. Many persons thought another long female reign undesirable. The Earl of Northumberland, in one of the letters now printed, says that the people wished for no more queens, fearing they should never enjoy another like Elizabeth.[a]

[a] Page 55.

Others regarded Arabella's want of definiteness in religion with dislike. It was understood that, in despair of the success of persons more absolutely desirable, the Pope had recommended that Arabella should be adopted as the claimant to be supported by the Roman Catholics; and, without openly professing Roman Catholicism, she was thought to be inclined that way, and to be certainly willing to make favourable terms with the Roman Catholics.

If, perplexed with these considerations, inquirers were inclined to throw aside the line of Scotland and resort to that of Suffolk, there were many difficulties. To say nothing of doubts as to the validity of the marriage of Mary the sister of Henry VIII. with Charles Brandon Duke of Suffolk, Catherine Grey, the eldest representative of that marriage, had secretly married the eldest son of the Protector Somerset. Her eldest son was Edward Lord Beauchamp. If legitimate, he was the heir of the house of Suffolk, and of the throne under the will of Henry VIII. But was the marriage of his parents valid? Was he legitimate? The question had been litigated. Popular opinion was probably in his favour, but such legal decisions as had been given were against him. He had, moreover, made a marriage of disparagement, which had involved him in much trouble. Was that a family in which to seek an heir to the throne?

If it were concluded that Lord Beauchamp was illegitimate, the right of the House of Suffolk was vested in the representative of Catherine Grey's sister, who was the Earl of Derby; but he was of course liable to question in reference to the legality of the marriage of Mary Queen of France and Charles Brandon.

If, confounded by these multitudinous difficulties, all the descendants of Henry VII. were thrown aside, the uncertainty was not diminished. Partisans were found for the Earl of Huntingdon, a representative of the Duke of Clarence of malmsey-butt memory, brother of Edward IV., and eight other persons were put forth as descended from Edward III., among whom were several foreign princes. The roll of pretenders was closed with the most powerful, and, in that sense, the most formidable, of the whole, the King of Spain, Philip II., and his daughter the Infanta Isabella Clara Eugenia, wife of the Archduke Albert, the Governor of Flanders.

The ultramontane Roman Catholics busily fomented the bewilderment which seemed to hang around this multiplicity of titles. It was their care to exaggerate the difficulties of the question, and to multiply possible pretensions. No less than fourteen titles were in this manner " idly or mischievously reckoned up."[a]

It seemed as if the uncertainty which was thus generated must be most pernicious. It unquestionably gave schemers and persons of faction ground for disturbing the present quiet, and it looked as if it must be full of danger for the future. Why then, it may well be asked, was not the question brought forward and settled in Parliament, especially as, after the death of Mary Queen of Scots, there would have been little difficulty in doing so? The only answer is, that this course was forborne out of respect to the decidedly adverse opinion of Queen Elizabeth. It has been asserted that she abhorred to be reminded that she was mortal. But Lord Bacon has emphatically declared this opinion to be utterly untrue; "for very often, many years before her death, she would pleasantly call herself an old woman, and would talk of the kind of epitaph she would like to have upon her tomb."[b] Her objection was of another kind. She feared that the indication of her successor might expose her to the mortification of beholding her own glory wane before the lustre of the rising sun. It seems probable, also, that she had some vague notion of her own prerogative right, as the last of a certain line of princes, to indicate her successor by her will. But such was the intensity which age gave to her feeling

---

[a] Hallam, Const. Hist. i. 389; and see a Treatise on the State of England by Wilson. [Dom. Corr. State Paper Office, 1600.] Wilson was contented with twelve claimants.
[b] Works, vol. vi. p. 312, of the admirable edition of Mr. Spedding.

against any approach to the subject, that neither they who were personally the most intimate with her, nor they who were the most entirely trusted by her in the management of public affairs, dared venture to raise so great a storm as would have ensued from soliciting her to give her mind to the consideration of the proper disposition of so vast a trust.

But, in truth, the public inconvenience resulting from humouring the personal feeling of the aged Queen was nothing like so great as might have been anticipated. Injustice to the several claimants there was none, and uncertainty there was really none, except in the minds of overheated partisans. The people settled the case at their own firesides. Unseduced by the cavils or quibbles of Jesuits or lawyers, their common sense threw aside the difficulties piled up before them, and seized at once upon the true principle of a right determination. The line of Henry VIII. was about to fail. They must go back to Henry VII. James of Scotland was Henry VII's eldest lineal representative, his true and obvious and nearest heir. Building upon that foundation, the judgment of the vast majority of the people—it may be said, the judgment of the nation—was clearly in his favour. Without polling-place or show of hands, without affronting the weakness of the Queen by a public discussion, the opinion passed from homestead to homestead by the electrical influence of an obviously right judgment, until from the Land's End to Berwick there was substantially but one opinion. The Jesuit who pretended that he found very few who favoured the title of the King of Scots, enabled people, as Mr. Hallam has well remarked, by the impudence of that assertion to "appreciate his veracity," whilst the stricter religious party among the Protestants merely exhibited, as they have too frequently done, a distrust in their own power and the power of their principles, and an over-fear of their opponents, by clamouring for a parliamentary recognition of a decision which was already concurred in by every one.

The only persons who were really deceived by this state of things were to be found in foreign nations. Ignorant of English people as English people were of them, and deriving their knowledge of the circumstances principally from religious exiles and enthusiasts, who had everything to gain from commotion, foreign nations supposed that on the death of Elizabeth there was to be a scramble for the Crown of England; that, as once before in the course of our history, the symbol of royalty would hang upon a bush to be seized by the victor on some future field of Bosworth. It was not in the nature of Englishmen to treat such folly otherwise than with silence.

But there were some persons, as has been already hinted, who were likely to pervert such a state of things for factious or ambitious ends; and this consideration brings us into contact with one of the principal subjects of the present volume.

The two leading men in England at that time were among the most remarkable persons of their age. They were men also whom nature seemed to have formed in every thing by way of opposites. Robert Earl of Essex was in person tall and well proportioned, a man of able body, and of lofty bearing, although with a remarkable bending forward of the neck, and a curious want of grace in walking or dancing. He was especially distinguished, as all observers have chronicled, by the true aristocratic mark of hands " incomparably fair." Sir Robert Cecil, on the contrary, was considerably below the ordinary stature; he was deformed, and altogether undistinguished by any special grace or dignity, either of feature or person. The statue on his tomb in Hatfield Church represents him as boyish, if not almost dwarfish, in height and general appearance. In manners and ordinary conduct the contrast was equally striking. Essex was what in those days was termed " full of humours," wayward, uncertain, impatient, fantastic, capricious; acting by fits and starts, upon impulses and prejudices; but ever with a dash and brilliancy that were nearly allied to genius. Sir

Robert Cecil was his very contrary in all these respects. Brought up at the feet of his pre-eminent father, he acquired, perhaps inherited, the highest official qualities; a calm, quiet, patient thoughtfulness, the power of mastering and applying details however intricate; diligence that was never weary, patience that could not be exhausted, temper that was seldom ruffled, and a habit of comparing, and sifting, and weighing, and balancing, which generally led him to right conclusions. Essex was generous in the highest degree, a patron of literature, and of all noble and gentle arts, and ever ready to take the lead in kind and liberal deeds; he was at the same time impetuous, fiery, vehement,—a man of action; courageous, daring, and more than anything delighted with military command, and with the *éclat* and brilliancy of a soldier's life. Cecil was a man of thought and law and peace, neither a soldier himself nor looking upon war in any shape save as a necessity to be deplored. Consciousness of his own physical defects kept the one man comparatively humble; consciousness of his own power of dazzling and attracting people, and of attaching them to himself, puffed up the other, and led him into continual extravagances.

Sound judgment in the transaction of business was Cecil's greatest quality, and, after a few years' experience of his eminent ability in that respect, there not only gathered round him a knot of attached public men, or, as we should term them, a "political party," but the people came to look upon him as a man to be safely trusted and confidently followed. The influence of Essex extended to a far wider and more enthusiastically attached gathering. His early favour with the Queen, his uncertain standing in her estimation—now hot now cold—and his own romantic character, created and kept alive a general interest in his fortunes, which he was careful to increase by constant endeavours after popularity. This last was his weakest point. He sought popular favour; at first, probably, without any other design than that of enjoying the consciousness of being well thought of; but when this end had been often enough attained, when he felt and knew himself to be the idol of the soldiery and of the people, and beyond all question the most popular man in England, his mind opened to the charm of a nation's applause, and the peculiar situation of the kingdom inspired him with an ambition which, according to his views and the state of things at the time, could only be accomplished by treason against the present possessor of the throne. Here again there is another most striking contrast between Essex and Cecil. The principle of loyalty in Cecil was fixed in his very heart of hearts. No circumstances can be conceived which could ever have tempted him to fail in his allegiance. He had been brought up in a school in which the sovereign was regarded as the sacred embodiment of an almost divine authority, and in which obedience was rendered instinctively, like some natural action with reference to which doubt or question is almost without meaning. In Elizabeth's case there were other and peculiar considerations which weighed heavily with Cecil. Her age, her sex, the many great qualities she had exhibited throughout her reign, and the obligations she had laid upon himself and his family were all remembered and set in the balance against the occasional mortifications which resulted from the frowardness and the obstinacy of her old age. Essex's loyalty partook of the fitful uncertainty of his general character. He had received from the mere favour of the Queen honours innumerable, and gifts which were valued at 300,000*l*. His memory of these benefits was written in water. When it was his cue to be loyal, no man could exceed him in professions of attachment; but, no sooner did the Queen's wishes or opinions run counter to his feelings, than he was loyal only to himself.

In questions of public policy, it was scarcely possible for two such men to agree. If Sir Robert Cecil had been a statesman of pre-eminent genius, intellect would have vindicated its power, and Essex would have taken his place as a member of a government in which Sir Robert Cecil was the head. As it was, they stood in the arena as competitors, and it was in their final struggle that the question of the succession was really determined.

That struggle was brought on by the death of Lord Burghley. Essex aspired to step into his position. The thought was mere madness. It shows how little knowledge he possessed either of himself or of the Queen. From early life his overbearing disposition had been a continual source of trouble to his royal patron; she could not but know that, as principal minister, the man whom as a court minion she had found it impossible to govern would have been her master; and he ought to have observed that in no part of her administration had the Queen exhibited more accuracy of judgment, or more absolute determination of will, than in her selection of the fittest persons for her official advisers. The Queen preferred Sir Robert Cecil, and thenceforward Essex's feud with him became irreconcileable. Even before the appointments were actually made, although it can scarcely be said that they hung in doubt, Essex's mind was full of projects of the most dangerous character. Office was his aim, not because its trammels would have suited his taste or its duties his capacity, but because it would have given him power which, like the Queen's past benefits, would have been "wings to his ambition."[a] He had "a settled opinion that the Queen could be brought to nothing but by a kind of necessity and authority."[b] The only way by which it seems to have occurred to him that he could acquire such authority as was necessary to induce her, or rather to compel her, to appoint him to the desired offices was by an open display of military

---

[a] Bacon's Works, vi. 300, ed. Montagu. [b] Ibid. p. 251.

power, or in other words by an armed rebellion. All his schemes tended to that point; but even armed rebellion, if it design to be popular, which it must be in order to be successful, must assign a cause, and one of a general character and interest. A purely selfish plea, even in the case of the rebellion of an Essex, would never pass muster with the people. Essex deemed that he found the required cause in the unsettled state of the question of the succession. He drew a veil over himself and his own pretensions and alleged grievances, and set abroad or adopted the monstrous fiction that Cecil and the members of the government were favourable to the title of the Infanta, that they were pensioners of Spain, and were ready to sell the country to the daughter of Philip II.

To avert so frightful a calamity, Essex was ready at all risks to take the field. His object was to drive these iniquitous and unpatriotic ministers from the councils of the Queen. It was his further intention, as soon as the reins of government were in his hands, to call a parliament in which the ejected ministers should receive their due punishment, and an act be passed for the regulation of the succession to the Crown.

The minute details of Essex's plots are now most difficult to be recovered, and that for various reasons. The common practice of the government at that period to omit from the depositions given in evidence all such passages as were unnecessary with a view to a legal conviction, or which it was impolitic to make known, has in this case been a peculiar barrier to historical inquiry. The criminal facts of which Essex was ultimately convicted, the treasonable conferences at Drury House, and the consequent London outbreak—to which the depositions used upon his trial were principally applied—constituted but a very small portion of his plot. They were the last crowning acts of folly, but they were only the sequence and result of various previous schemes, all of them not less absurd. It is in these previous schemes that the true clue to his intentions is to be found. But they did not come in question legally at his trial, and the little information we find respecting them in the proceedings on that occasion is altogether unsatisfactory and inconclusive. What then appeared in reference to them rather slipped out than was made known intentionally; what remained behind in the partially used depositions, or in depositions altogether unused, was purposely kept back because it implicated persons not before the court, and in some cases persons of such station and importance that even the government could not venture to call their acts in question. One of these persons was Lord Montjoy, Essex's successor in the government of Ireland, and then successfully employed in putting down that rebellion of Tyrone with which Essex had failed to cope. Another person was King James of Scotland, the almost acknowledged successor to the crown. The government could scarcely throw suspicion upon him, unless they were prepared to move for his exclusion from the succession. Another reason why they would desire to conceal the actions of these two persons, probably was that one, if not both of them, had really given the government more or less information of Essex's dangerous designs. The same reason no doubt applied to other persons. And there was still another reason, that the information which was obtained by the government came out gradually, and much of it after Essex had been beheaded, so that the opportunity of using it in the public proceedings against him was not afforded.

The circumstances under which the fuller information was obtained are worthy of being borne in mind. Essex had evidently hoped that his fate would have been determined upon the simple evidence of his endeavour to rouse the citizens to join him in a movement against the Court. In that case, the only point in his case would have been, what was the legal character of his conduct on that occasion? But the government had carried the inquiry farther back, and on his trial examinations were read of several of his principal friends in which they had disclosed certain preliminary conferences, in which the course ultimately endeavoured to be acted out had been resolved upon. These disclosures filled Essex with indignation. He viewed them as acts of treachery, and before he left Westminster Hall, with his accustomed impetuosity and want of consideration, returned counter accusations against his friends, and began to play against them the game which he suspected they had put in action against himself. His indignation, aided perhaps by religious considerations infused into his mind by an attendant chaplain, led him to make disclosures exceedingly damaging to those of his friends who yet remained to be tried, and implicating persons who up to that time had not been suspected. He even urged his secretary, Cuffe, upon whom he ungenerously laid the principal blame of his own misdoings, to imitate his example and disburden his conscience by means similar to those which he had himself adopted. The results may be conceived. Essex himself wrote something in the nature of a confession, contained in four sheets of paper, and others of his accomplices followed his example with willing pens. The feelings of the time with reference to this conduct may be judged from the following extract from a contemporary letter of George Carleton to his brother Dudley, the future Secretary of State:[a]

" It was strange to see the beginning of this action (whereof I was a beholder) and somewhat strange to consider the circumstances now toward the end. For these noble and resolute men, assured of one another by their undoubted valour, and combined together by firm oaths, being all taken, severed, examined, and the principals arraigned and condemned, fell in the end before their deaths to such plain confessions and accusations one of another, that they seemed to strive who should draw one another in deepest; and sought by all means to remove the blame and shame of being the first movers and

[a] State Paper Office, Domestic, 1601, March 25.

contrivers of these their confessed treasonable plots one from another, in which the Earl himself exceeded all other, to all men's wonder. For he accused Cuffe, Sir Christopher Blunt, &c. to be his motors; they excused themselves; Sir Christopher Blunt flatly accused him to have entered into consultation at his being in Ireland for the bringing in of 4000 of the Queen's soldiers then under his commandment with him, with full purpose to right himself by force, of such wrongs as he complained he had received here in his absence, unto which there were none made privy but the Earl of Essex, the Earl of Southampton, and himself; which course he avouched at his death had been put in execution, had he not earnestly, and the Earl of Southampton in some measure, dissuaded. Further the Earl of Essex of his voluntary confession accused Sir Henry Neville, Lord Ambassador for France, to be privy and a party to this confederacy, as they term it, of Drury House (where the secret conventicles were kept for three months together before the action, at the least,) whom no man did dream upon, in this case. Whereupon he was presently sent for back again, being in his journey toward France as far as Dover, examined, and committed; and his confessions served to accuse others. The like with most of the rest. Sir John Davis is thought to have saved his life with telling first, who otherwise was in with the deepest."

The curious information obtained by this general humour of confessing has been but partly made applicable to our history. Some of it is to be found in the State Paper Office, but still more among those papers from Hatfield which have been placed at the disposal of the Camden Society for the purposes of the present volume. I have thought that it would be appropriate to our present subject, and most useful to future historians, if such of these confessions as in any way affect the King of Scotland were added to this volume. In some cases, only a passage here and there in a long examination has that bearing, but partial publication of such papers is always unsatisfactory. I have preferred, therefore, to print the whole in an Appendix.

As my object is not to write a history of the Essex conspiracy, it will suffice that I point attention to these documents, and notice their contents so far as they relate to King James. It seems clear that Essex had been in correspondence with that sovereign for a considerable time, certainly from the year 1598.[a] His letters were written, as Cuffe states, from a desire to keep King James stedfast in his Protestantism, then popularly esteemed doubtful, and to concert measures for counteracting the designs of the presumed friends of the Infanta, that is, the members of the Queen's government. James answered these letters, but neither letters nor answers are known to be in existence. Shortly after Essex's return from Ireland, he was committed, as is well known, to the custody of the Lord Keeper. Essex's friend, Lord Montjoy, anxious for his safety, wrote to King James soliciting his interference. James replied by a messenger, that he " would think of it, and put himself in a readiness to take any good occasion." Montjoy, in the depth of his solicitude for the fate of his friend, and urged by Essex to do something for his extrication,—probably also being at the time under the maddening influence of his passion for Essex's sister, sent his Scottish Majesty " a project," as it was termed, the effect of which was that James should prepare an army, should march at the head of it to the Borders, should thence fulminate a demand to the English government, of an open declaration of his right to the succession, should support the demand by sending an ambassador into England, and of course, although not so stated, if his demand were refused, should cross the Borders as an invader.

To this notable scheme of a northern armed demonstration, Montjoy added a proposal on his own part, that, being now about to go to

[a] Cuffe, Appendix, p. 86.

Ireland as Lord Deputy, he would bring over from that country one-half of the Queen's army, sent thither to suppress the rebellion of Tyrone, by way of supporting the demand of the Scottish monarch. Essex was also to raise his friends within the kingdom; and the union of the Irish invaders with the army of Essex, together with the aid to be derived from the Scottish demonstration or invasion, was calculated upon as sufficient to effect the designed purpose. All this was proposed, and was to be enacted, amidst the customary protestations of a reservation of duty to her Majesty, and all possible respect to the claims of allegiance. The Earl of Southampton informs us, that he wrote to James with an offer to support this preposterous scheme with his "endeavours and his person." The reply of the peaceful James is declared by the Earl of Southampton to have been one of acceptance—"he liked the course well, and would prepare himself for it." (Appendix, p. 97.) Sir Charles Danvers alleges, with more likelihood, that it was one of evasion, either that he was not ready, or that he could not declare himself until the Irish troops were at Lough Foyle prepared to embark for England.

In the mean time Essex, for whose benefit the dangerous project had been suggested, was partially released, and for the time the scheme fell to the ground. After some months, the Queen, being probably partly acquainted with some of these treasonable plottings, still continued to regard Essex with disfavour. She would not admit him to her presence, notwithstanding his many protestations of fidelity and affection. Her firmness excited his impatience, whilst the arrest by the government of the messenger who had been sent on his behalf into Scotland alarmed him. In his fear of some great discovery he called upon his friends again to rouse themselves on his behalf. The Earl of Southampton, an impressionable person, full of flighty notions, and evidently as weak as water, was sent into Ireland to propose to Montjoy a partial revival of his former project. King James was for the present left out of the calculation. Sir Charles Danvers, whom Essex much relied upon, thought that the Irish troops, with the addition of the contingent of the Earl of Essex, would be sufficient for the contemplated purpose, and Southampton was commissioned to express to Montjoy the solicitude of Essex that the army from Ireland should be landed in Wales as soon as possible. But Southampton found things greatly changed with Montjoy. As the Queen's representative in Ireland, with a clear perception of the onerous responsibilities which were attached to that position, and full practical experience of the serious difficulties and responsibilities connected with rebellion in any shape —removed also from the influence of Essex and of Essex's sister— his judgment had regained its clearness. He saw what ruin he had narrowly escaped, and determined no longer to play with weapons so dangerous and so dishonourable. "He utterly rejected it," are the words of the Earl of Southampton, "as a thing which he could no way think honest, and dissuaded me from thinking of any more such courses. . . . . . I do protest also before God, I left the Deputy (as I thought and so I assure myself) resolved to do her Majesty the best service he could, and repenting that he had ever thought that which might offend her."[a]

Montjoy endeavoured to find an excuse for his past folly in the circumstance that he had previously been acting, or proposing to act, in conjunction with the presumptive heir to the throne. "He thought it more lawful," is the account of Sir Charles Danvers, professedly derived from Montjoy himself, "to enter into such a cause with one that had an interest in the succession than otherwise, and though he had been led before, out of the opinion he had to do his country good by the establishment of the succession, and to deliver my Lord of Essex out of the danger he was in, yet now his

[a] Appendix, p. 97.

life appeared to be safe, to restore his fortune only, and save himself from the danger which hung over him by the discovery of the former project, and to satisfy my Lord of Essex's private ambition, he would not enter into an enterprise of that nature."[a]

Again there was a pause in these treasonable speculations. Lord Deputy Montjoy suggested to the Queen's government that his friend Southampton—no less repentant than himself—should be appointed Governor of Connaught. The Queen and Sir Robert Cecil were too well acquainted with the nature of their past transactions to concur in any such appointment. Southampton was rejected, and withdrew into the Low Countries.

But the fire in the heart of Essex was unquenchable. The last fatal project of forcing himself into the Queen's presence by a *coup d'état*, and violently assuming the reins of government in her name, broke upon him. The foolish and unprincipled persons whom he gathered about him encouraged the idea; all means were used to increase his popularity. The "people were persuaded that none was careful of them but he; the soldiers, that none considered their preferment but he;" to "the purer sort in religion" he appealed by seeming more religious than others; to the Roman Catholics by expressions in favour of toleration and the withdrawal of penalties. All the customary artifices of demagogues were used by him and all around him. Mr. John Littleton, of the family since worthily ennobled, was sent over into the Low Countries to tempt Southampton to return home and take part in the plot. The representations addressed to him are stated by Southampton in his letter before referred to (Appendix, p. 97). They are perhaps a little too highly coloured; but, whatever was the nature of Littleton's mission, it is unquestionable that it brought Southampton back to England to run with Essex that career which led one of them to the scaffold, and the other so close to it that his escape seemed almost a miracle.

[a] Danvers, pp. 103, 104.

Essex would again have applied to Montjoy for the troops to be landed in Wales; but being assured of the inutility of any such proposal, he limited his request to a letter in which Montjoy should complain of the ill government of the State, and express his wish that some course might be taken to remove her Majesty's bad advisers. Southampton declared that Montjoy would not write any such letter—" there was no spirit in him towards any such course;" and if Montjoy had been totally free from the weakness of his father, who ruined himself and his family by the vain pursuit of alchemy, he would peremptorily have rejected such a proposal. But the fascination of Essex kept him in awe, and, although he protested against his schemes, and urged him to patience, and the use of ordinary means to recover the Queen's favour, he told him, that if he would needs have a letter from him, he would send him such a one as he could justify. Either this was not the kind of letter which Essex desired, or the *dénouement* came on too rapidly, for no letter seems ever to have been written.

The King of Scotland, the other party to the original scheme of the three armies, was not forgotten. A letter to him was debated and finally agreed upon about Christmas time in 1600, by the Earls of Essex and Southampton, Sir Charles Danvers, and Cuffe. The purport of only one part of it appears. That was to urge the King to send up the Earl of Mar to London, by the first of February, as an ambassador to the Queen; but to act, in that character, in concert with the Earl of Essex, so as to promote the objects of some contemplated movement. Essex and his friends knew, by this time, that the government was watching them with eagles' eyes.[a] It was difficult therefore to communicate with King James by any messenger who should not excite suspicion. Such a messenger was

---

[a] The expression is Sir Robert Cecil's (State Paper Office, Dom. Feb. 13, 1600-1), but was applied by him to the suspicious scrutiny with which the proceedings of Essex were watched in Ireland.

found in a person who is described as "Norton the bookseller," not Bonham Norton, but his cousin who stands in the list of printers as "John Norton, Esquire." This Esquire printer kept shop in St. Paul's Churchyard, and had business connections with Scotland, which would render his journey to Edinburgh in the dead of winter less liable to suspicion. He had very lately been engaged in the republication of a book of public interest,[a] originally printed in Scotland, by royal command. Cuffe, it will be seen, leaves him a legacy in his will (printed in the Appendix, p. 92), and mentions him in terms which almost lead to the inference that he had induced Norton to lend himself to this dangerous employment. Norton received Essex's letter at Berwick from the hands of Lord Willoughby, the Queen's governor of that town,— how conveyed to him, or whether with his knowledge of the contents, does not appear. Norton was to deliver it to the Scottish King, and his Majesty was solicited to return his answer " in disguised words of [*i.e.* relating to] three books," which it is said he did. The scribe who penned the examination from which we quote, began to write the names of the three books which were disguisedly to stand in place perhaps of those of Essex, King James, and the Earl of Mar; but having written thus far, " vizt. Garric Lonyes," he desisted and struck his pen through what he had written. The last word is confused by the attempt at cancellation, and is difficult to be made out; I am not sure that I read it accurately. The word " Garric " may perhaps mean " Gowrie," and have reference to the account published of the Gowrie conspiracy.

James's answer has not been found, nor have I discovered any allusion to its contents. We may conclude that it was to a certain

---

[a] " A Discoverie of the unnatural and traiterous Conspiracie of Scottish Papists against God and his Church . . . set down as it was confessed by Maister George Ker and David Graham of Feutrie." Lond. 4to. 1593. The book related to the conspiracy known as that of the " Spanish Blanks."

extent favourable—first, because it was preserved by Essex with great care; and secondly, because, in consequence of Essex's request, the Earl of Mar was expected to arrive, and did actually arrive, in London, although not at the time appointed.

The point of the Earl's careful preservation of King James's letter is thus made out. Several of the examinations indicate that Essex was accustomed to wear round his neck a small black taffeta bag, or purse, for it is called by both names. In this purse he kept, as he himself says, " a paper, which contained not in quantity above a quarter of a sheet, and in it there was not above six or seven lines." He further described it as " an advertisement sent unto him, and not of his own hand, but written by another man."[a] All this very well describes what James's answer may have been, and Cuffe distinctly says that the answer of the King of Scots " was it which the Earl carried about him in a black purse." Southampton asserts the same thing. The Earl himself, when interrogated on the subject, declared, that on his return to Essex House, after his failure in the City, he took the paper out of the bag and threw it into the fire, in the presence of his wife and sister, and the lords, knights, and gentlemen who were then with him. The government, deeply interested in tracing out and securing the evidence of every ramification of the conspiracy, especially so far as related to King James, directed Sir John Peyton, the Lieutenant of the Tower, to search the person and clothes of the Earl for the black bag. Sir John's report of the way in which he performed his disagreeable duty, couched in terms of jailor-like particularity, will be found in the Appendix, p. 80. The search was entirely unproductive, and was conclusive against the Earl's having any such bag in his possession whilst in the Tower. Edward Bushell, it should be added, one of the persons examined in reference to the conspiracy, and who was probably the first to give information respecting this

[a] Peyton, Appendix, p. 81.

black bag, stated, that when the Earl came back to Essex House he said, "that if a black purse [originally written 'bag,'] he had about his neck were found, it should appear by that was in it, how he was betrayed in the City." Both accounts are probably true; the Scottish letter may have been ordinarily and principally kept in the bag; but some paper, received at the last moment, perhaps from Sheriff Smyth, who was Essex's principal reliance in the City, may have been temporarily deposited there. There can be little doubt that, whatever were the contents of the bag, they were presumed by Essex to be inculpatory of the writer, or writers, if there were really two papers, or of himself, and that Essex destroyed them on the occasion above mentioned. His rebellion of a day having miserably failed, and his fate staring him in the face, he consigned to the flames many papers over and above those in the black purse. Besides the written paper or papers, the purse contained the key of a little iron chest, in which there was "a book of his troubles, all written with his own hand." He had also another "little iron chest," of which the key was lost. He broke it open, and took out "divers private papers and letters that no man's eye ever saw but his own"—perhaps letters from the Queen—and destroyed them all, together with the book of his troubles, and the contents of the black purse.

The fact that the Earl of Mar was expected by Essex, is unquestionable. Essex prepared a paper of instructions for him, of which Cuffe gives the main particulars, in Appendix, p. 82. It states, at considerable length, the assumed facts from which Essex inferred, or would have had the King of Scots infer, that the members of the Queen's government were in a conspiracy against his interest. From one of Cuffe's letters, it also appears that it was the Earl's intention to send " some well-qualified confidant " to meet the Earl of Mar before his arrival in London. The object of this confidant would have been to understand " the full resolution of the principal party from whom he [Mar] was sent," and, according as it was found to be thoroughly favourable to Essex's views, or not, so Mar was to be dealt with. If Mar's instructions from King James were such as Essex desired, the part which the ambassador was to play in London was clearly defined for him by Essex in these instructions.

I cannot doubt that the arrival of Mar and his coadjutor—for James joined with him in his embassy Mr. Edward Bruce, the titular abbot of Kinloss, a lawyer of eminence in the Scottish courts—was purposely delayed. They left Edinburgh about the middle of February, with a train of forty persons. Such a cavalcade at that time of the year travelled slowly. Essex was executed on the 25th February. It was well into March before the Earl of Mar and his companions reached London.

In that interval an extraordinary change had taken place in the state of England, and in the position of the question of the succession; but, blinded by the representations of Essex, full of deep-seated prejudices, and living at a distance from the scene of action, James comprehended little of the real character of the new position in which he was placed. He was infinitely grieved for the fate of Essex. It was in vain that those about him pointed out that the popular Earl would have been as dangerous to the hopes of the presumptive successor as he was to the peace of the actual sovereign. James termed him his martyr, and expressed himself strongly against Sir Robert Cecil, whom he still believed to be his enemy. In James's second instructions to the Earl of Mar and his fellow ambassador, written after the death of Essex,[a] he proceeds upon the supposition that there was a serious disagreement between the Queen and the people. He instructs his ambassadors how to finesse according to the nature of this disagree-

---

[a] Their first instructions written before that event have not been found.

ment, and the prospect of a consequent rebellion. He directs them to crave of the Queen and Council, or, as he more frequently terms them, " the present guiders," the release of all persons imprisoned for going into Scotland without licence, and a declaration to be entered of record that he was untouched by any action or practice ever intended against her Majesty, especially by that of Essex; also to solicit them to put a difference between those of her subjects who dealt with him and those that practised with her greatest enemies; also that the Queen would liberally consider of his necessities, and would bear in mind her old promise not to do anything in prejudice of his future right. On these heads he directed them to assure Mr. Secretary and her principal guiders that if the King found his requests answered, he would make account of their affections towards him accordingly. He authorised his ambassadors in that case to give them full assurance of his favour, " especially to Mr. Secretary, who is king there in effect." If they could get nothing but a flat and obstinate denial to all their requests, "which," he says, "I do surely look for," he directs them to inform the Queen that he should pray to God to open her eyes, and to let her see how far she was wronged by such base instruments about her as abused her ear, and that, although he should never give her occasion of grief, yet the day might come when he would crave account of her ministers of their presumption, and when there should be no bar betwixt him and them; "and ye shall plainly declare," he proceeds, "to Mr. Secretary and his followers, that since now, when they are in their kingdom, they will thus misknow me, when the chance shall turn I shall cast a deaf ear to their requests; and whereas now I would have been content to have given them, by your means, a pre-assurance of my favour if at this time they had pressed to deserve the same, so now, they contemning it, may be assured never hereafter to be heard, but all the Queen's hard usage of me to be hereafter craved at their hands; and thus shall ye part, without any just offence to the Queen, please the humour of the people, and use no greater threatenings than such as I shall be very able to perform in the own time."ᵃ

These instructions have been praised as an exhibition of King James's sound judgment and clear apprehension; they rather indicate his want of information, and folly. They are a manifestation of the spirit which had been raised by Essex, and, if acted upon, would have gone far to have been fatal to King James's hopes of succession. That the ambassadors of a prince who had been mainly kept on his throne by Elizabeth, and for many years had received a handsome annuity from her bounty—a prince who owed her respect, if not allegiance, as the head of his house—should have been instructed to address her in the language which is above quoted, and that, among other reasons, in order to buy popularity, or, as it is termed, to please the humour of the people, and thus to pave the way to the throne, was an act of almost incredible want of wisdom. It was fortunate for James that his ambassadors were wiser or had better means of observation than himself.

A few days' residence in London must have convinced them of the necessity of adopting a very different course. They would there have learned that the asserted support of the Spanish title by Sir Robert Cecil had been proved to be a wild and monstrous fiction, by one of the most striking incidents in our history. It occurred in court on Essex's trial. Credulous in the belief of anything which told against his opponents, Essex justified his declaration, made openly in the streets of London, that the Crown of England was sold to the Spaniard, by asserting that he had been told that Sir Robert Cecil had said to one of his fellow-councillors that the Infanta's title was as good as that of any other person. On the instant, Cecil, who had been sitting within ear-shot, but in some

---

ᵃ Lord Hailes's Secret Correspondence, pp. 9, 10.

place where he was hidden from observation, stepped forth into the open court. Dropping on his knee to the honourable tribunal, he begged permission to answer "so foul and false a report."[a] The Lord Steward and others of the peers made light of Essex's accusation; but Sir Robert persisted in his request, and in a speech of vehement eloquence challenged Essex to name the councillor to whom he was stated to have spoken those words: "Name him, if you dare; if you do not name him, it must be believed a fiction!" Essex, thus openly challenged, turned to his fellow-prisoner, the Earl of Southampton, and vouched him as having heard the assertion as well as himself. Cecil appealed to Southampton, by all the love and friendship that had been between them from their tender years, by the honour of his family and house, and by his Christian profession, to name the suggested councillor. After a little hesitation, Southampton indicated Sir William Knollys, an uncle of the Earl of Essex, and the Comptroller of the Household. Cecil entreated that a messenger might instantly be despatched to the Queen to command Sir William's immediate attendance in Westminster Hall. Mr. Knevet was directed to wait upon the Queen accordingly, Cecil charging him, "as he was a gentleman and tendered his reputation," not to acquaint Mr. Comptroller with the cause of his being needed, and to assure the Queen, that if either out of her care for Cecil's reputation, or out of her love to Mr. Comptroller, who was her relative, her aunt Mary Boleyn's grandson, she denied to send him, Cecil vowed upon his salvation that he would never again serve her as a councillor while he lived. The cause proceeded during Knevet's absence. In due time he returned into a crowded court, in which every heart must have fluttered with anxiety. He came accompanied by Sir William Knollys. Sir William stood forward. This was the critical moment of Essex's fate, no less than that of Cecil. The answer would be the ruin of

[a] Jardine's Criminal Trials, i. 353.

one of them. What a breathless hush must there have been among the crowded and excited auditory! No need to pray silence in the court. The lawyers stood aside whilst the cause was being determined upon an issue which they had not raised. The Lord Steward put the question, " Did Mr. Secretary ever use any such speeches in your hearing, or to your knowledge?" The answer was prompt and decisive: " I never heard him speak any words to that effect!" The reply must have fallen upon Essex like the stroke of the axe. But there was something more. Sir William proceeded: " There was a seditious book written by one Doleman, which very corruptly disputed the title of the succession, inferring it as lawful to the Infanta of Spain as any other; and Mr. Secretary and I being in talk about the book, Mr. Secretary spake to this effect: 'Is it not strange impudence in that Doleman to give an equal right in the succession to the Crown to the Infanta of Spain as any other?' Hereupon was grounded the slander upon Mr. Secretary, whereof he is as clear as any man here present." The witness returned to his attendance in the palace. Essex apologised, but his cause was lost; his principal pretence for rebellion was cut from under him, the chief link which bound him to the hearts of his adherents was severed, he stood before them the champion of a lie. " I confess I have said," added Cecil, with scarcely more than allowable triumph, " I have said that the King of Spain is a competitor of the Crown of England, and that the King of Scots is a competitor, and my lord of Essex I have said is a competitor; for he would depose the Queen, and call a parliament, and so be king himself; but as to my affection to advance the Spanish title to England, I am so far from it, that my mind is astonished to think of it, and I pray God to consume me where I stand, if I hate not the Spaniard as much as any man living!"

In this incident there was far better instruction for the ambassadors of King James than in the paper dictated by his own petulance and misinformation. They soon found it to be so. Cecil had refuted the Essex slander, he had repudiated the King of Spain, but the question remained—whom did he favour? The juxtaposition in which he had placed the King of Scots in the passage just quoted seemed almost to answer the question; but could not an explicit declaration be drawn from him? The Scottish ambassadors determined to try. Cecil favoured their attempt. His situation had been materially altered by the removal of Essex. In England his power had been greatly increased; towards Scotland he stood in a new position. The influence of his opponent had ceased, the untruths circulated against him, merely, as Essex is said to have admitted in his confession, *ad faciendum populum*, had been swept away. James could now, therefore, be fairly approached, and there were circumstances which rendered such approach desirable—the Queen's growing infirmities; the fussy anxiety and curious self-conceit of James, which laid him open to deceits and misleadings on all hands; and the fact that Essex's death had not removed all those who sought to derive personal advantage from intrigues in reference to the succession. It is clear that, although upon Cecil's principles a parliamentary recognition of James's title could not be obtained, it was for the benefit of the country that an understanding with him should be come to by those upon whom would devolve the business of taking the practical initiative in reference to his succession. To have left all that was then to be done to the last moment, and to the haphazard determination of the Queen's dying hour, would have been both unstatesmanlike and unpatriotic. Regard for the Queen's feeling, or folly, if it pleases any body so to term it, rendered it necessary that the understanding should be private; but regard for the public and the country rendered it imperative that there should be an understanding. Since Sir Robert Cecil's appointment as head of the ministry, no opportunity until this time had been offered for anything of the kind. It came now, and he took advantage of it.

A meeting was held between Cecil and the ambassadors, apparently on their request, at the Duchy House; that is, the house of the Duchy of Lancaster in the Strand. Probably some cause of conference was assigned in reference to James's solicitation for an increase to his allowance, or to his claim of the right of succession to the lands of his paternal grandmother, Margaret Countess of Lennox. However that may be, the conference was held, overtures were made to Cecil by James's ambassadors, he replied to them without disguise, and thence ensued the understanding out of which sprang the following letters.

Among Cecil's terms stipulated with the ambassadors were the following:—

1. That an absolute respect should be paid to the feelings of the Queen, and therefore that there should be a cessation of all endeavours on the part of King James to procure any parliamentary or other recognition of his right to the succession; and

2. That all intercourse between Cecil and the King should be kept an inviolable secret, so that it might never reach the ears of the Queen, with whom it would be a subject of misconstruction and an occasion of the deepest offence against both parties.

In order to carry out these terms of arrangement, a series of numbers, which should represent the principal persons whose names were likely to be introduced in any communication by or on the part of Cecil or James, was agreed upon, and these numbers will be found to be used throughout the following Correspondence:—

   0 was The Earl of Northumberland.
   2 ,, Sir Walter Raleigh [?].
   3 ,, Lord Henry Howard.
   7 ,, Lord Cobham.
   8 ,, Mr. Edward Bruce.
   9 ,, Mr. David Foulis.
   10 ,, Sir Robert Cecil.

20 was The Earl of Mar.
24 ,, Queen Elizabeth.
30 ,, King James.
40 ,, A colleague of Cecil's, but who has not been discovered.

The report which Mar and Bruce made to their sovereign of the results of this important conference was quickly followed by the first of these secret letters, addressed by King James to Cecil. James commended, it will be seen, Cecil's plain and honourable dealing with his ambassadors, and suggested that Lord Henry Howard, whom he recommended to Cecil in terms which indicate that he did not suppose that Lord Henry had hitherto been much in Cecil's confidence, should be the " sure and secret interpreter " between them. Out of Cecil's concurrence in this suggestion arose that correspondence which was published at Edinburgh in 1766, in a small 12mo volume, under the title of " The Secret Correspondence of Sir Robert Cecil with James VI. King of Scotland."

The letters thus published are unquestionably genuine. They agree in every way with those now brought to light, and, although all written by or to Lord Henry Howard, in a certain sense they constituted a "secret correspondence" between James and Cecil; but they were not their only nor their principal secret correspondence. The letters now published were the only correspondence which can with strict propriety be so entitled.

It is not my intention to dwell on the contents of the letters now published. They speak for themselves, and must be read by all persons who desire to understand this incident in our history, or the feelings of the several parties; but I cannot refrain from pointing attention to the second letter, which is Cecil's first direct address to his royal correspondent. It contains an explanation of his past conduct, a vindication of the step taken by him in opening up this secret communication, a full assurance of the state of the Queen's mind, and plain advice with respect to James's future conduct. In all these points the letter alluded to will be found clear and satisfactory. Cecil's vindication against the accusations of Essex had been effected before the correspondence was opened. That James believed him to have been wronged by Essex, and promised henceforth not to credit adverse rumours without inquiry of himself, constituted the foundation of Cecil's whole proceeding. For the future, he entreats the King to quiet his thoughts in reference to the Queen, to dismiss from his mind all apprehension that she entertained any alienation of heart from him, and to pluck up by the roots any notion that she was inclined to " cut off the natural branch and graft upon some wild stock;" he warns him of endeavours made by many persons to prejudice the Queen against him, and urges the adoption of clear and temperate courses to secure her Majesty's heart, " to whose sex and quality nothing is so improper as either needless expostulations or over-much curiosity in her own actions." He assures the anxious King that so long as he keeps from urging his pretensions he may sleep secure, so far as concerns the Queen. Above all things, he cautions him against being over busy and anxious to prepare the people for the coming event. The whole letter deserves the most careful attention and study. As an indication of the course of policy recommended by Cecil to James, and from this time acted upon by him, it is peculiarly valuable. In that view, it fully establishes for Cecil the honour of having, by his advice and management, brought his aged sovereign to the grave in domestic peace and with untarnished lustre, and secured the transference of the crown from the house of Tudor to that of Stuart with the same tranquillity that it might have passed from father to son.[a]

The correspondence began between March and June, 1601. During the two years that elapsed between the former of those dates and the death of Queen Elizabeth, all the letters now published were

[a] Hume, cap. xlv.

written. Throughout that time it is obvious that there was a gradual but steady increase in Cecil's influence, not only in England, but over the flighty self-conceited James. His Majesty's eyes were at length opened to the danger of Essex's plottings. He learned to write of him as "a noble gentleman," but one in whom he " lost no great friend " (p. 65). On the other hand, Cecil's solid business qualities won their way, until from intense dislike the King passed to the most ardent admiration. He came to see how entirely the minister's policy, neither blind nor overtrusting, but persistently quiet and quieting, was surely working in the direction which his Majesty desired to steer. There was something, too, in the mystery of the correspondence, and the little plots and concealments and evasions and denials to which both parties had recourse in order to secure their secret, which was quite to the King's taste. It smacked of the statecraft which was then too generally practised by all parties, and was pretty nearly King James's idea of the perfection of wisdom. Sometimes an occasional doubt came over him. He longed to be doing something to widen or to strengthen, as he thought, his foundations, and the correspondence now published, as well as other letters which passed from 1601 to 1603 between Cecil and Nicolson, and the Master of Gray, and which exist in the State Paper Office or at Hatfield, show that Cecil occasionally found it difficult to repress the disposition to make surety doubly sure, which was natural under James's circumstances, as well as the unwise and unwary gossip in which it was part of his nature to engage.

The secret of this correspondence was well preserved. Known to half a dozen persons (King James, Cecil, Lord Henry Howard, the Earl of Mar, Bruce, and Foulis), and probably to several others, nothing ever occurred to betray it to any of the inquisitive persons by whom the leading parties were surrounded. James, on one occasion, dropped unwary words, which Nicolson, the English agent in Scotland, instantly caught up and communicated to Cecil. A strong denial written by Cecil to Nicolson in reply, in a form designed to be communicated to the King, either put an end to Nicolson's suspicions, or demonstrated to him, as well as to James, that the subject was not one to be talked about. Many persons suspected that there was an understanding between the King and the minister, but no accident ever revealed its exact character. A well-known story, which stands upon the authority, excellent in many respects, of Sir Henry Wotton, and by him asserted to be " precisely true,"[a] proves the hazard of detection which Cecil occasionally ran, and the ease with which he could extricate himself by a stroke of mother-wit. " The Queen," says Wotton, " having for a good while not heard any thing from Scotland, and being thirsty of news, it fell out that her Majesty, going to take the air towards the Heath (the Court being then at Greenwich), and Master Secretary Cecil then attending her, a post came crossing by and blew his horn. The Queen, out of curiosity, asked him from whence the despatch came, and being answered ' From Scotland,' she stops the coach and calleth for the packet. The Secretary, though he knew there were in it some letters from his correspondents, which to discover were as so many serpents, yet made more show of diligence than of doubt to obey, and asks some one that stood by (forsooth in great haste), for a knife to cut up the packet (for otherwise he might have awaked a little apprehension); but in the mean time approaching with the packet in his hand, at a pretty distance from the Queen, he telleth her it looked and smelt ill-favouredly, coming out of a filthy budget, and that it should be fit first to open and air it, because he knew she was averse from ill scents. And so, being dismissed home, he got leisure by this seasonable shift to sever what he would not have seen."

Cecil's eyes seem to have been ever open to the possibility of his correspondence coming to the knowledge of the Queen. His

---

[a] Reliq. Wotton. p. 169, ed. 1672.

letters now published were clearly written with that idea in his mind, and he was careful to keep about him persons who could be trusted with a secret of such importance, or those who had not wit enough to draw inferences from what they might possibly see going on around them. An instance in proof of this occurred in July 1602. Cecil had at that time a Secretary named Simon Willis, a man of ability, but a pushing, excitable, ambitious person. Of a sudden he was dismissed. The cause privately assigned was "insolence and harsh behaviour"[a] to his master; but Willis, justifying his dismissal, went to Rome, and, with the accustomed zeal of such converts, strove to make himself conspicuous, and of use to his new church. Half-a-dozen years afterwards, when James was well seated on his English throne, Cecil was desirous to ascertain something of Willis's doings at Rome, and wrote upon the subject to Sir Henry Wotton, then ambassador from England to Venice. He prefaced his letter thus:—

"You know Simon Willis, whom, about a year before the Queen died, I discharged of my service, partly for his pride, whom provender had pricked, but principally because I was loath he should have come to some discovery of that correspondency which I had with the King our Sovereign, which without great difficulty I could not have avoided, considering his daily and near attendance as my Secretary, to whose eyes a packet or a paper might have been so visible, as he might have raised some such inferences thereof as might have bred some jealousy in the Queen's mind, if she had known it, or heard any such suspicion to move from him. Wherein, although I hope you remain secure, if her Majesty had known all I did, how well these [she?] should have known the innocency and constancy of my present faith, yet her age and orbity, joined to the jealousy of her sex, might have moved her to think ill of that

[a] Chamberlain's Letters during the reign of Elizabeth, edited by Miss Williams for the Camden Society, pp. 151, 154.

which helped to preserve her. For what could more quiet the expectation of a successor, so many ways invited to jealousy, than when he saw her ministry, that were most inward with her, wholly bent to accommodate the present actions of the state for his future safety, when God should see his time?" He further assured him that this cause of Willis's putting away was known to most of those great men with whom in this correspondence he was associated, and then proceeded to the main purpose of his letter, which is not connected with our present subject.[a]

Some persons, who may be presumed to have known more or less of the correspondence, are indicated by the seals still remaining attached to many of the letters now published. In only one case, and that not a royal letter (p. 52), is there a seal which clearly belonged to the King himself. The others are seals of Sir Thomas Erskine (afterwards Earl of Kellie), Patrick Young, David Foulis, and Edward Bruce, all well known persons in connection with the royal household, or with this correspondence. It would seem to have been the King's practice, in reference to his letters to Cecil, to use the seal of some member of his household, acquainted with the secret, who chanced to be in attendance upon him at the moment when the letter was despatched.[b]

It is a curious subject of speculation in what way letters of such great importance and secrecy were conveyed from London to Edinburgh. The ordinary mode of government conveyance was that described by Sir Henry Wotton. The packet, inclosed in a budget or wallet, was carried by a special messenger who rode post, that is, on horses furnished by the postmasters at the ordinary stage towns, and accompanied by a guide or servant of the postmaster, who

---

[a] Collins's Sydney Papers, ii. 326.

[b] In describing and identifying these seals, I have had the great advantage of the assistance of Thomas William King, Esq., York Herald. His perfect acquaintance with all heraldic subjects, and the zeal with which he aids literary inquirers, cannot be too frequently commemorated.

attended to the hired horses on the road, and after the traveller had completed his stage brought them back to the place of departure. Such a mode of conveyance, at a time when men are presumed to have been rough and unscrupulous, and over such roads as then existed, seems as if it must have been dangerous and exposed to many chances. Private travellers no doubt sometimes got roughly handled, and the ordinary messenger or letter-carrier of the postmaster was occasionally waylaid and robbed of a particular letter or packet, but my recollection does not supply me with any instance of the stoppage or loss of a government packet conveyed in the way that I have indicated. Still, I cannot think that these letters were forwarded by any common channels. Letters to Edinburgh passed ordinarily through Berwick, and the messengers were subjected to inquiry by the government authorities of that Border garrison. Certainly these letters did not go to George Nicolson, the ordinary English agent in Scotland (the "pigeon" of this correspondence and that published by Lord Hailes), for delivery to the Scottish King. A government messenger bringing letters to any other person than Nicolson, would have given occasion to more suspicion and inquiry than any of the parties to this correspondence would have desired to excite. I incline therefore to the supposition that they must have been conveyed by special and secret messengers, and probably by or through diplomatic agents of the Scottish sovereign, not ordinarily carriers of letters.

It has been asserted that they were conveyed round by Dublin, a mode of transit which seems full of difficulties. It is true that the messenger going that route would not be liable to the same suspicion as he would if taking the direct road to Edinburgh; but such a roundabout way must have added immensely to the danger and the chances of accident. It must have been as difficult to get the letters to Dublin as to Edinburgh, if not more so. In Dublin, James had certainly two trusty agents—Mr. James Hamilton and Mr. James Fullerton, two Scotchmen connected

INTRODUCTION.

with Trinity College, Dublin. Hamilton was the eldest of the six adventurous sons of Hans Hamilton of Dunlop, who all sought fortune in Ireland, and founded families in that country, members of several of which have been ennobled. Fullerton's origin was humble, but both were men of learning, and both, for several years before the death of Elizabeth, were in direct communication with the court of Scotland as political agents. The story told about them is, that they were sent into Ireland by King James in the year 1587, to keep alive and advance his interests in that country. The better to disguise their object, they established a school in Dublin, and took upon them the places of master and usher. Among their pupils they had the honour of numbering the illustrious Usher, afterwards Archbishop of Armagh. On the establishment of Trinity College, Dublin, Hamilton was appointed a Fellow, and in that capacity continued his tutorship of Usher, who followed him to Trinity College in 1593, at the age of thirteen. Hamilton was much employed in the affairs of the College and of his master King James, and is traceable in the correspondence of the period, now in Scotland, now in Ireland, now in England. He was anxious to have arranged with the English government for the employment of Scottish troops in Ireland against Tyrone, and was recommended to effect that object by Sir Richard Bingham, who praised his honest carriage and loyal demeanour, and described him as having lived in Ireland with the good liking and commendation of the State and best-affected.[a] It is perfectly possible that he may have been one of the messengers employed in the transmission of this secret correspondence, and there was a tradition that he was so. The rewards heaped upon him very shortly after James's accession, indicate that his services had been of a kind which were deemed to have deserved ample recompense. Weighty grants to him are quoted from the Patent Rolls, ultimately culminating in his elevation to the peerage in 1622, by the titles of Lord Hamilton

[a] Ireland, State Paper Office, 1600, Feb. 1.

and Viscount Claneboy. He survived until the 23rd January, 1643-4.[a]

The usher Fullerton's services are not so obvious; but after James's accession he removed to England, and not only attained to high offices about the Court, but procured also some of those convenient grants which courtiers generally managed to appropriate to themselves. The last office held by him was that of Groom of the Stole to Charles I., said to have been worth 2,500*l.* per annum.[b] He died in January, 1630-1, and was interred in Westminster Abbey by torchlight, his body being accompanied from his house in Broad Street by a procession of one hundred coaches. A news-writer, in communicating the intelligence, remarks, "Little did he think of such grandeur when he was usher of the Free School in Dublin, and Sir James Hamilton, since created Viscount Claneboy, and now one of the greatest subjects in that kingdom, schoolmaster, where they laid the first foundation of their fortune, in the latter end of Queen Elizabeth's reign, by conveying the letters of some great lords of England, who worshipped the rising sun, to King James, and his letters back to them; this way of obliquity being chosen as more safe than the direct northern road."[c] Here, at any event, we have the tradition.[d]

Among the Scottish agents of the highest class who may have been similarly employed, David Foulis was probably one. He came with the Earl of Mar and Bruce as their secretary, and was several

---

[a] Lodge's Peerage, ed. Archdall, iii. 1; and Strype's Life of Sir Thomas Smith, p. 137.

[b] Court and Times of Charles I., ii. 89.

[c] Court and Times, ii. 89, 90. Fullerton's punning epitaph was, I suppose, written by Fuller.

[d] Bishop Goodman says that "the correspondency was ever sent by the French post, and not by Berwick," which seems more improbable than the asserted transmission by way of Ireland. The Bishop follows this statement with a singular perversion of the story quoted at p. xxxix. from Wotton. It is evident that he had not any accurate information upon the subject. (Court of James I. i. 32.)

times sent to London to receive the allowance paid to James by Queen Elizabeth. He attained his reward in estates in Yorkshire, but fell under the displeasure of Lord Wentworth, the subsequent Earl of Strafford, and the censure of the Court of Star Chamber, in the reign of Charles I.

As the time drew on for the realisation of James's long-cherished hopes—when, according to his own figure, he was to change the wild unruly colt which it had been his hard and wearisome business to manage, for the towardly riding horse which was ridden by St. George (p. 31)—his anxiety and that of his friends increased. As early as November, 1599, when, under the blinding influence of Essex, and almost regardless of the goodwill of Elizabeth, or the maintenance of a good understanding with her Ministers, then supposed to be Spanishly affected, James procured it to be suggested to his principal nobility of Scotland that they should enter into a league or "Band" for the preservation of his person, and the pursuit of his right to the crowns of England and Ireland. Such an engagement was accordingly entered into. He also solicited from his Parliament, perhaps in connection with the Montjoy plot of the three armies, which had just been proposed to him, a liberal grant for warlike purposes in reference to the succession. "He was not certain," he told them, "how soon he should have to use arms; but whenever it should be, he knew his right, and would venture crown and all for it".[a] The Scottish burghers gave no support to these wild and foolish schemes, calculated only to irritate Elizabeth, to render James himself unpopular in England, and to play the game of Essex.[b]

---

[a] Scotland, State Paper Office, Dec. 15, 1559. Nicolson to Cecil.

[b] The Bond entered into by the Scottish nobility attracted little attention in England, although well enough known. Chamberlain notices it as an article of news in a letter to Dudley Carleton, dated 22 Feb. 1600. See Chamberlain's Letters during the Reign of Queen Elizabeth, edited by Miss Williams for the Camden Society, p. 66.

After the fall of Essex, and the understanding with Cecil, all James's tactics were changed. He became the most affectionate of relations to the Queen. To disturb the amity between them was a thing not to be dreamed of. "With what mask or veil," he asks, could I cover that blot to mine honour, in being the first breaker of (for an untimely ambition) that long-continued friendship betwixt the Queen and me, especially at this time when, by my long honest behaviour towards her, I have at last attained to a more inward and confident amity with her than ever was betwixt us heretofore?" (pp. 62, 63.)

The idea of employing arms against England was shocking to him. "He could neither be religious, wise, nor honest," to do anything of the kind. "How," he innocently inquires, "could I be religious to prevent God's leisure by unlawful anticipation, and to do that wrong to my neighbour the like whereof I would be loth to suffer in my own person? It were very small wisdom by climbing of ditches and hedges for pulling of unripe fruit, to hazard the breaking of my neck, when by a little patience and abiding the season, I may with far more ease and safety enter the gate of the garden, and enjoy the fruits at my pleasure in the time of their greatest maturity." In these quaint similes we see the evidence and the results of Cecil's influence.

But some of his gentry, who were not in the secret, did not display anything like the King's calmness and equanimity. Ignorant of his actual position, they even thought to win his favour by exhibiting their zeal for his unrecognised rights. An example occurs in a letter of Nicolson's, in Vol. 92, No. 130 (2), of the Hatfield letters, which may be quoted as an unpublished evidence of the fact. This letter is dated "Brighen [Brechin], the 16 of April, 1602." Nicolson writes—

"The King remaynes still in these partes feasted vp and downe the contry, and very kyndely caryenge me with him, and playenge at mawe against Mr. Lepton and me. At his being at Kynnarde he was well entertayned and welcomed, where in drinck the larde of the house thought he should have pleased the King by drinckinge to the joyninge of thes two kingdomes in one, and soone, and sayeing he had forty muskitt ready for the Kinges service to that vse; which the King saide was a faulte in him to wish soone, or by force, and protested he wished no haste but Godes tyme in it, and her Majestie's daies to be longe and happie without any abridgment of them or howre of them, for any cause or kingdom to him; prayeng God if he wished otherwaies in the secrett of his harte, that he neuer enjoyed his owne kingdome or life, with many good wordes of her Majesty, and protestacones that he looked not for it by force but by right, when that day should come, and with fauor of the people and not as a conqueror. And, by the way, in his goinge from thence to Montrosse, he protested in his discourse with me, his vpright and true harte to her Majesty to be neuer to wishe or know her hurte but to reveale it as God should judge him, and that as her kynsman and commed of her Majesty he aught her and would performe her alleageance, and would be subject and answere her as her subject so in any thing, albeit as King of Scotland he was not so bounde; with many other better wordes then I can write, acquiting her Majesty of the Queen his mothers deathe freely. The King intends to write his thanckes to her Majesty and is still impeded, but within few daies will do it. I se him of that good mynde as I can not wish him better, nor do thinck there is any thinge in his powre that he may pleasure her Majesty in that he will not willingly do, so well affected is he now to her Majesty. He staid in thes partes huntinge, but with mynde also to reconsile Murray and Huntlay, and to have them at the baptisme, where the younge Prince[a] I thinck shall not now be; in this tyme also he is doinge justice and agreinge other quarrells in this contry."

[a] Prince Henry.

INTRODUCTION.

The papers at Hatfield give much information respecting the final illness of the Queen, and the movements in consequence, both in England and Scotland. The way in which Cecil secured the success of his plans for the peaceable accession of the successor, may be clearly gathered from his own papers.

The Queen's illness assumed a decided character early in March, 1602-3. Want of sleep was its first and most continuous symptom, accompanied by weakness and exhaustion. "I am not sick, I feel no pain," she said of herself; "and yet I pine away."[a] The news spread like wildfire, and with it all kinds of rumours and speculations. The citizens were warned to pay attention to watch and ward, and it appears, from a letter of Sir John Carey, Lieutenant-Governor of Berwick, to Sir Robert Cecil, that as early as the third of March, either Sir Robert himself or some one whose letter was inclosed in the government packet for Scotland, apprised Sir John "of my Lady of Nottingham's death, and of her Majesty's not having been well." Sir John had long been striving to get leave of absence to come up to the Court—partly, probably, to seek instructions with reference to coming events. It was now, he judged, too late to solicit such permission. With the Queen ill, it was out of the question for him to quit his government. He must, he says, "arm himself with patience perforce."[b] On the 9th March, matters had so far advanced that Sir Robert Cecil took the initiative more decidedly. He wrote to Nicolson in Edinburgh the following letter, which is printed from a draft or copy in the handwriting of Levinus Monck, probably dictated to him by Sir Robert.

MR. NICHOLSON,

Although booth the last packetts served for convoye of other mens letters, and this haue noe other great perticuler occasion, yet because I would not haue you ignorant of those thinges which

---

[a] Ellis's Letters, 2nd Ser iii. 194.   [b] Hatfield MSS. vol. xcii No. 19.

are like enough by bruict to passe into that kyngdome, especially concerninge matter of that nature wherof I now must write, I haue thought it my part to acquaynt you as followeth: First, it is trew that till within these ten or twelve dayes I never beheld other shew of sickenes in the Queen, then meerely those thinges that are proper to age; Next, that now, her Majesty, thankes be to God, is free from any perill; but because all fleshe is subiect to mortallity, and that all her creatures can never ymagyne to [her?] to die, or fear to much when ought concerneth her, I must confesse vnto you, that she hath been soe ill disposed theise eight or nyne dayes, as I am fearefull least the contynuance of such accidents should bringe her Majesty to future weakenes, and soe to be in danger of that which I hope myne eyes shall never see; for although she hath good appetite, hath nether cough nor fever, distemper nor inordinate desyre to drincke, yet she is troubled with a heate in her brestes and drynes in her mouth and tongue, which keepes her from sleepe every night, greatly to her disquiett. And this is all, whatsoever you hear otherwise; for which she never keept her bedd, but was within theise three dayes in the garden. For all other matters I must referr you to the next, and soe committ you to God's proteccon."[a]

About the 13th of March it was rumoured that the Queen was better. On the day following, Lord Cobham wrote to Cecil from his house in the Black Friars, expressing his hope to hear from Cecil " the continuance and assuredness of her Majesty's recovery."[b] The amendment was merely a flash of lightning. On the 16th, Sir John Carey writes to Cecil, from Berwick: " I despatched away your last letter to Master Nicolson into Scotland presently, which went in good tyme, for that there came post with the same packett a gentleman of Scotland, called Master Alexander Morrey, who came a thorrowe post from London, although he deneyed it hear,

---

[a] Hatfield MSS. vol. xcii. No. 18 (2).   [b] Ibid. No. 33.

and brought with him letters of her Majesty's being verey ill; but your packett was at Edenborrowghe befor he came ther, wherbey Master Nicolson had the first knolledge, wiche the retorne of his packett will fortefey you. Honorabell Sir, youer last letter to me, with the report of Master Morrey, hathe sett suche a grefe so neer my hart as I fear will not eseley be removed, styll doutinge the worst."[a] Nicolson writes the same day from Edinburgh that he was comforted by Cecil's last, and that he prayed for her Majesty's " yet good and many days . . . albeit some other do advertise secretly otherways."[b] The "some other" were probably the correspondents of whose letters Alexander Murray was the bearer.

On the 17th March, the Earl of Rutland, who had been in the Essex outbreak, writes from Belvoir, that Lady Howard had sent him word that the Queen had promised that he should see her and kiss her hand—a parting token of reconciliation; but that the report of her indisposition was no less grievous than the former was comfortable. He would pray for her recovery as for his own soul.[c] On the same day was written from London a letter of the Earl of Northumberland to King James, which will be found at p. 72, and which gives one of the best accounts in general terms of the Queen's illness. She had then been ill almost a month; for the first twelve days her indisposition was kept secret, under the mistaken notion that annoyances in public affairs and the death of Lady Nottingham were the occasion, and that time would restore the patient. These anticipations had totally failed. Sleep and appetite had forsaken her. For twenty days she had scarcely slept at all. Physic she would take none, and serious apprehensions began to be entertained. In these grave circumstances the Council had called upon Lord Thomas Howard, Lord Cobham, and the Earl of Northumberland (being all the noblemen, besides the Council themselves, then in London), to

---

[a] Hatfield MSS. Vol. xcii. No. 42.   [b] Ibid. No. 43.   [c] Ibid. No. 46.

INTRODUCTION.

give their assistance in consultation, and the result was that the Earl became daily more and more convinced of the power of the Secretary, and that he was friendly to King James. "If your Majesty can win him sure to you, you shall give a great hope to your business, and to all our cases."

On the 19th March, Nicolson writes that the accustomed musters of King James's household had been put off for this time, and a contemplated northern journey with a French ambassador been turned into a Stirling journey to see the young prince.[a] On the same day Sir Robert Cecil's elder brother Lord Burghley, Lord President of the North, addressed him in a very remarkable letter:—" My desyre is now," he says, " after so manny days paste, to know what is to be lookyd for. Her Majesties yeres consyderyd can beare no vyolent nor long sycknes. But pryncypally my wrytyng is to know from yow what course yow think fittest for me to hold, for that yow know best what is to be intendyd . . . . whether to come uppe or to go northward. Here I doo intend to make my randevouse to be ready ethar way as occasyon shalbe offryd. For I thank God I can remayne strong in booth places, by authorityc in thone place, and by love and frendes in these partes. I only doo relye uppon God's prouydence, but yett I thank God not vnprovyded booth of men, horse, and weapons, to defend the ryght, to the which God direct our myndes; and I hope though we may be farr dystant in myles, yet we shall concurr ' in one harte and in one waye,' as yow repetyd, thembleme of hym that is gone."[b] The allusion is of course to their illustrious father, and to his motto, " *Cor unum, via una,*" still retained by the elder branch of his descendants. On the same day, probably, Sir Robert Cecil forwarded to King James a copy of the intended proclamation of his accession (p. 47); and Sir Robert Carey despatched a messenger from Richmond, where the Queen was lying

---

[a] Hatfield MSS. Vol. xcii. No. 47.   [b] Ibid. No. 47 (2).

past all hope. The messenger had audience of King James in his bed at seven in the morning, and delivered his tidings. The Queen, it was affirmed, could not outlive three days; and Sir Robert Carey, in anticipation of that journey which brought him fame and fortune, had already placed horses along the Northern road, that he might be the first to bring the King the news of his accession.

By the 21st the rumour ran that the Queen was *in extremis*. The tide now flowed strong towards the North, and the letters here published picture vividly the arrival of successive messengers, and the feverish impatience of King James. Throughout England uncertainty and agitation were becoming extreme. Sir John Carey, either craftily, or in utter ignorance of what was to ensue, suggested to Sir Robert Cecil the propriety of fortifying Berwick, and furnishing him, as governor, with victual and munitions. He pictured the wonderful discontent and desperate murmurs of the Scots at rumours that the Lady Arabella was about to be married, and foolishly revived his request to be allowed to come up and be the better resolved how to discharge his duty.[a]

As the real crisis approached, offers of service and assistance flowed in, some to the Council, and some to Sir Robert Cecil individually. Official people were bewildered as to what they were to do, and Lord Burghley and Sir John Carey were not the only persons who wished to have a few private words with Sir Robert Cecil;—the last thing which Cecil would permit. The Lieutenant of the Tower, if I understand rightly the following letter, was as much puzzled and as distrustful as any one. He had already been in communication with King James, who entertained a very exalted idea of his importance, perhaps derived from some conjectured similarity between the situation in reference to the metropolis of the Tower of

---

[a] Hatfield MSS. Vol. xcii. No. 53.

INTRODUCTION.

London, and that of Edinburgh Castle. At sunset on the night of the 22nd March, some directions were sent to Sir John Peyton by the Council, perhaps relating to his prisoners. Some clue to their purport may perhaps be guessed from the following mysterious letter which was his reply:—

"RIGHT HONORABLE,

"Yesternight, at the shutting of the gates, I receyued your honors letters, having then neither tyme nor means to return answere, as to me in duty appertayned. Tocheing the matter informed, I doe assure me selfe, that in your honorable judgements your [honors] wylle conceyve, that I am not so voyde of respect as to immagin that singulalarytyc or disorder can geue any advancement vnto meryte, leauing those hasty cowrses onely to be vsed in suche cases wher ther is an opposytion agaynst right intended, the which I am sure is as farre remoued from every of your honors reasolutions, as it is from myne to doe eny thing that maye preiudys your honorable opinions of me. Most humbly takeing me leaue. Your honors to doe you all scruyss.
JOHN PEYTON.

Towre, this 23 of March, 1602."

[*Addressed,*]
"To the right honorable, my very good lords, the lords and others of her majestyes most honorable pryvye Councell."*

When the Tower gates were next closed after the date of that letter, the Queen was lying in utter unconsciousness. At midnight she fell into a slumber, the state which she had so long desired, but had found to be unattainable. After a couple of hours she awoke, but it was only to die. At three o'clock the consummation had been attained. She had ceased to breathe.

For days and weeks past much public business had been utterly

---

* Hatfield MSS. Vol. xcii. No. 65.

paralysed. Now of a sudden all was bustle and activity. The members of the Council who had stood round the Sovereign as she sank to rest shortly afterwards dispersed. Posting to London, the doors of Whitehall opened for them as the grey dawn of a March morning began to appear. Summonses were issued to other persons whose presence was desired. At six o'clock, as the sun rose, they assembled in the Council Chamber. Cecil produced the proclamation which had sounded so harmoniously in the ears of James. It was read and settled. If any one spoke of making terms, the analogy of an heir succeeding to a patrimony, was the answer. At ten o'clock the ceremony of proclamation was commenced at Whitehall Gate, at eleven it was repeated at the Cross in Cheapside, and that same night printed copies of the proclamation were transmitted to the new Sovereign. Before he received them the voice of the nation had fully ratified the act of the Council; the will of Henry VIII. had been set aside; all questions respecting inheritable blood had been passed over; James the First was in full possession, and the act of statesmanship of Sir Robert Cecil was complete. In his own words, he had steered King James's ship into the right harbour, without cross of wave or tide that could have overturned a cock-boat.

The present volume originated in two purchases, one made by the Camden Society, and the other by the Editor, of transcripts made many years ago of some of the letters now published. Those transcripts were found to be imperfect, and an application was made to the Marquis of Salisbury, through the noble President of the Camden Society, to know whether he possessed the originals from which the transcripts had been made, and whether, in that case, he would permit the Camden Society's transcripts to be collated. The Marquis answered the appeal made to him in the most liberal spirit. Anxious that any publication which might possibly affect the reputation for statesmanship of his ancestor Sir Robert Cecil, should represent the actual truth, the Marquis placed in the hands of the Editor, for the use of the Society, the whole of the invaluable originals of the Secret Correspondence, with other papers bearing upon the subject. The Camden Society, and all lovers of historical truth, will, I am sure, properly appreciate an act of such kind and judicious liberality.

JOHN BRUCE.

5, *Upper Gloucester Street, Dorset Square,*
    5*th March,* 1861.

CORRESPONDENCE

OF

KING JAMES VI. OF SCOTLAND,

RESPECTING HIS SUCCESSION TO THE THRONE OF ENGLAND.

PART I.

CORRESPONDENCE WITH SIR ROBERT CECIL.

No. I.

30 [KING JAMES] to 10 [SECRETARY CECIL.]

[HATFIELD MSS. VOL. CXXXV. FOL. 54.   ORIG. AUTOGRAPH.]

I ame most hairtelie glaid that 10 [Sec. Cecil] hath nou at last maid choice of tuo so fitt and confident ministeris* quhom with he hath bene so honorablie plaine in the affaires of 30 [K. James], assuring 10 [Sec. Cecil] that 30 [K. James] puttis more confidence in thaime, according to the large and long proofe that he hath had of thaime, then in any other that followis him, lyke as 10 [Sec. Cecil] is most beholden unto thaime for the honorable reporte that thay haue maid of him to 30 [K. James], quhomto thay haue, upon the perrel of thaire credit, geuin full assurance of the sinceritie of 10 [Sec. Cecil]; and because 30 [K. James] can not haue the occasion to speake face to face with 10 [K. James], that, out of his owin mouthe, he may giue him full assurance of his thankefull acceptance of his plaine and honorable dealing, he thairfore prayes 10 [Sec. Cecil], to accepte of his long aproued and trustie 3 [Lord Henry

---

* John seventh Earl of Mar, and Mr. Edward Bruce, afterwards Lord Kinloss, sent by King James as ambassadors to Queen Elizabeth in February 1601.

Howard],* both as a suretie of his thankefulnes and his constant loue to him in all tymes hearafter, as also to be a sure and secreate interpretoure betwixt 30 [K. James] and 10 [Sec. Cecil], in the opening up of euerie one of thaire myndis to another; quhom 10 [Sec. Cecil] hath the bettir cause to lyke of and truste, since, long before this tyme, 3 [Lord Henry Howard] dealt uerrie earnistlie with 30 [K. James] to take a goode conceate of 10 [Sec. Cecil], offering him self to be a dealer betuixt thaime, quhair upon 30 [K. James] was contentid that 3 [Lord Henry Howard] shoulde deale betuixt essex and 10 [Sec. Cecil] for a conformitie betuixt thaime, for the uell of 30 [King James] in the owin tyme,† but that 10 [Sec. Cecil] mistrusted the aspyring mynde of essex, 30 [K. James] can not but comend, taking it for a sure signe that 10 [Sec. Cecil] uoulde neuer allow that a subiect shoulde climbe to so hie a roume, and that he shoulde euer be thrall to a subiect that hath from his chyldehode bene trained up in the seruice of a free prince; and yett 30 [K. James] doth protest, upon his concience and honoure, that essex had neuer any dealing with him quhiche uas not most honorable and auouable. As for his misbehauioure thaire, it belongis not 30 [K. James] to iudge of it, for althoch 30 [K. James] loued him for his uertues, he uas no uayes obleished to embrace his querrellis, but to accepte of euerie man according to his owin desairtis. This farre hath 30 [K. James] thocht goode to comitte to paper, to be a uitnesse to 10 [Sec. Cecil] of his inuarde disposition touardis him, assuring him that he takes in uerrie goode pairt his warenes in dealing, lyke as he doth promeise, upon his honoure, that in all tymes hearcafter, the suspition or disgraceing of 10 [Sec. Cecil] shall touche 30 [K. James] as neare as 10 [Sec. Cecil], and quhen it shall please

* Second son of Surrey the poet. King James, shortly after his accession to the throne of England, advanced Lord Henry to the Earldom of Northampton, and subsequently conferred upon him the order of the garter, and other honours. Lord Henry inherited much of his father's ability, but degraded it by many vices. He won the heart of James by flattery almost unparalleled.

† This passage is printed as it stands in the original.

god that 30 [K. James] shall succeide to his richt, he shall no surelier succeide to the place then he shall succeide in bestowing as greate and greater fauoure upon 10 [Sec. Cecil] as his predecessoure doth bestow upon him, and in the meane tyme ye maye rest assured of the constant loue and secreatie of

Youre most louing and assurid freinde,

30 [KING JAMES].

[*Addressed in the King's handwriting.*]
" 10."

[The letter has been fastened in two places with pink silk, and sealed, also in two places, with a seal bearing for arms, a pale, charged with a crescent as a mark of cadency; and for crest, a crescent, between the horns of which is placed the letter T with the letter S on the dexter side of the crescent and the letter A on the sinister, probably the initials of Sir Thomas Aireskine, or Erskine, afterwards Earl of Kellie.]

[*Indorsed by Sec. Cecil,*]
" 1600. 30, first letter to 10." He has subsequently added in explanation of 30 and 10, " The K."; " Secretary."

No. II.

10 [SECRETARY CECIL] TO 30 [KING JAMES.]

[HATFIELD MSS. VOL. CXXXV. FOL. 55. COPY CORRECTED BY SEC. CECIL.]

May it please your Majesty,

Although it hath pleased you to lett me reade in royall characters, what the constitution of your mynde is towardes me, what you esteeme my disposition towardes you, and vppon what argumentes both your favour and opinion are and shalbe grounded (whereby I rest secure that an even measure hath been offered me by all those that haue handled that subiect), yet can I not deny my mynde that iustice which it exacteth from me, to be heard speake as much (with his proper organ) as hath been allready reported by other meanes. A desyre deriued from noe exception to the least article of their relations (of whom [*sic*] integritye and wisedome your Majesties lettres haue yeilded soe cleare demonstration), but only as a motive from those reverent respectes of myne which liue in doubt how silence would be censured to such a summons. In which consideration I haue resolued in this forme to retourne my humble thankes. First, because it hath pleased your Majesty to beleive that I haue been wronged. Secondly, because you expect nothinge from me to wrong any other. Thirdly, because you promise hereafter in all accusations to deale with me as God did with Adam, "*Vbi es?*" Fowerthly, because I perceaue when that naturall day shall come, wherein your feast may be lawfully proclaymed (which I doe wish may be long deferred) such shall appeare the equitye of your mynd to all men, as those shall not be reiected (as wantinge their wedding garment) whoe haue not falslye or vntymely wrought for future fortunes. For I doe herein truly and religiously profess before God, that if I could accuse my selfe to haue once imagined a thought which could amount to a grayne of eriour towardes my deare and precious souverayne, or could haue descerned (by the ouvertures of your ministers) that you had intertayned an opinion or desyre to draw me one poynct from my individuall center, I should wish with all my hart, that all I haue done, or shall doe, might be converted to my owne perdition. For, though it is trew that natural cares and providence might have importuned me long since, to seeke some honest meane to dissolue those hard obstructions which other mens practise had bredd within your hart, yet had I still determined constantly to haue runne out the glasse of tyme (thoughe with ideas of future perill), rather then by the least circumstance of my actions (ether open or priuate) to give any ground for insidious spiritts to suspect that I would varrye from the former compass of a sole dependencye, by which I haue only steered my courses.

But when I saw that all those whose eyes weare blynde to all but high imaginations, had left behynde them the dreggs of fowle impressions agaynst some ministers of this estate (especially agaynst my selfe, as one that was solde ouer to Spanish practise, and swollen to the chynn with other dangerous plottes agaynst your person), I did straight consider how necessarye it would be for me, if ether I desyred to keep my souveraynes cleare intentions from beeing blemished, or to quiett your thoughtes towardes her (in which the preservation of your future hopes (by consequence) is included), to plucke upp quickly by the rootes those gross inventions of my conspiracyes, because the multiplyinge still of such shaddowes vppon me (holdinge that place I doe) might prooue in tyme the cause of some effects verye preiudiciall to both your Majesties fortunes, the feare whereof hath been (I protest to God) the principall ground of my soe playne dealing with your embassadours. For when I perceaued that the practises which weare vsed to disgrace me, must consequently haue setteled an apprehension in you, of an alienation of hart in her Majesty towards you, which must have mortised an opinion in your mynde, that she must needes be inclyned (if not resolued) to cutt of the naturall branch, and graft vppon some wilde stocke, seeinge those that helde the neerest place about her weare described to be soe full of pernicious practises agaynst your Majesty, I did thinke it my dutye to remooue that inference, by that occasion which was offered me vppon your Embassadours beeinge here, though I assure my selfe (it beeing knowne) would preiudice me in her Majesties iudgment, of whom that language which would be tunable in other princes cares would iarr in hers, whose creature I am. But, Sir, I know it holdeth soe iust proportion, even with strictest loyaltye and soundest reason, for faythfull ministers to conceale sometyme booth thoughts and actions from Princes, when they are perswaded it is for their owne greater service, as albeit I did obserue the temperature of your mynde (in all your courses) to be such, as gaue me great hopes that you would doe allwayes like your selfe, yet I was still iealous, least some such causelesse dispayre of the Queenes iust intentions might be wrought into you, as might make you (though happelye not dissolue the mayne bond of honour and amitye), plonge your selfe vnawares into some such actions, as might ingage all honest men, out of present dutye, to oppose themselfes soe farr agaynst you, as they would stand in doubt hereafter what you would doe, in the future, towardes those which should soe lately haue offended you. Wherein I will only for the present lay downe this position, which I knuw I can iustly mayntayne, That it is, and wilbe, in noe mans power on earth, soe much as your owne, to be *faber fortunæ tuæ.*

And now must I leaue the quicke and resort to the dead,* of whom I would to God I could speake the best, seeing by your selfe his name was remembered, which is shortly this:—that if I could haue contracted such a freindship with him, as could haue giuen me securitye that his thoughtes and myne should haue been noe further distant then the disproportion of our fortunes, I should condemne my iudgment to haue willingly intruded my selfe into such an opcsition. For whoe know not that haue lived in Isaraell, that such weare the mutuall affections in our tender yeares, and soe many reciprocall benefittes interchanged in our growing fortunes, as besydes the rules of my owne poore discretion, which taught me how perilous it was for Secretarye Cecyll to haue a bitter feud† with an Erle Marshall of England, a Favorite, a Nobleman of eminent partes, and a Counsellour, all thinges els in the composition of my mynde did still concurr on my part to make me desyrous of his favour.

Thus haue I now *(ex mero officio* to my Souverayne, and out of affectionate care to your Majesties future happines, whom God hath instituted to sitt (in his dew tyme) in the chayre of state, at the feet whereof I dayly kneele,) exposed my self to more inconvenience then ether your Majesties former indisposition or my owne caution (in a iealous fortune) should adventure, seeing (by it) I doe reape noe other purchase then what I know your justice would yeild to all, which is to be only secured thus farr (in my owne honest and paynfull labours), that I shalbe censured by cleare and vpright prooffes, and not by borrowed lightes of envy and revenge.

It remayneth, therefore, that I draw toward an end of this tedious

* Of course the allusion in this very important passage is to the late Earl of Essex.
† This word has been altered and is a little doubtful.

lettre of myne, in which my affection must only couver my errours. Your Majesty knowes that iealousye stirreth passion, even between the father and the soonn, that passions begett iniuryes between Princes, and that iniuryes ether giuen or taken, in your case, breed alienation. To the first weaknes in her Majesties mynde I haue allready breefely sayd, That what was possible for art and industrye to effect, agaynst the person of a successour, in the mynde of a possessour, hath been in the highest proportion laboured by many agaynst you. Out of this conclusion, that the eyes of her Majesties suspition could not be diverted from other practises, vnles it weare ingrauen in her hart that you weare impacient of any longer attention. It beinge well knowne, that as love is of all thinges subiect to greatest blyndnesse, soe feare once multiplied nether trusteth profession, nor heareth reason. To resort therefore to my first groundes, your best approach towardes your greatest end, is by your Majesties cleare and temperate courses, to secure the heart of the Highest, to whose sex and qualitye nothinge is soe improper as ether needles expostulations, or over much curiositye in her owne actions. The first, shewinge vnquietnesse in your selfe; the second challendging some vntymely interest in hers; booth which, as they are best forborne when there is noe cause, soe be it farr from me (if there shalbe cause) to perswade you to receaue wronge and be sylent. Only this I dare say for the present (and that vppon good experience) that as longe as we see our horison cleare from lively apparitions of anticipation, your Majesty may *dormire securus*, for any counsell or humour rising from hence, of preiudice or prevention.

Further I must presume (vnder the former pardon) to say thus much to your Majesty;—that although it be a common rule with many rising princes to refuse noe adress, yet you will fynde it in your case, that a choyce election of a feaw in the present, wilbe of more vse then any generall acclamation of many; the one strengthninge selected and honest myndes when they see they are not reckned in the ordinarye (though they affect noe singularitye), the other having such a repugnancye in the mynde of her Majesty as those that resolue to be trew to booth, *in ordine*, shalbe forced to be more negligent of the second, least they should be mistrusted of lack of duty to the first. Whoesoeuer therfore perswades your Majesty that it is necessarie for you to be to busy,* to prepare the vulgar beforehand, little vnderstands the state of this question: nether shall your majesty fynde my woordes vntrew in this one thing more;—that if the extraordinarye persons (though small in number) whom nether base nor hawtye humours draw to love you, should fynde themselfes to be vsed as a motive to increase a publicke partye, (it being ordinarye for the vulgar to follow better example, without any such precedent insinuation,) suerly the myndes of men of spiritt and vallue are so compounded, the addition that is sought of the greater part, will be the privation of the other; *sed hoc nimis, hic posui baculum.* From my selfe and my † freind 3 [Lord Henry Howard] you shall not be combered with other petition, then that you will remember for your owne good (wherein I leaue to your iudgment to applie it to the right person) that noe man is soe very impious that travayleth not for some opinion of vertue. Next, that we doe nether presume to indent with you for future favours, nor present reseruidnesse, because we thinke it not ingenious to recommend to honour it selfe the thinges which honour requireth; with which conclusion I humbly kisse your royall handes, beeseechinge your Majesty to beleive that when I lived in deepest silence, your Majesty might then (as you may now) have iustly sayd vnto me (*usque ad aras*); *Cur non mecum loqueris, qui mecum sentis?*

[*Indorsed by Sec. Cecil,*]
A copye of my first lettre to the Kinges
  Majesty in the Queenes life, vppon my
  conference with the Erle of Marr and the
  Lord Kinlosse, at the Duchye House.

* The words " to be to busy " are an interlineation. The second " to " seems superfluous.
† " worthye " was struck out in revision.

No. III.

30 [KING JAMES] TO 10 [SECRETARY CECIL].

[HATFIELD MSS. VOL. CXXXV. FOL. 59. ORIG. AUTOGRAPH.]

Richt trustie and wellbelouit 10 [Sec. Cecil], If at my first dealing uith you by my laite ambassdouris, I had not bene setlid in that assurance that the partie I delt uith uas uise, and that my fauoure was to be groundit upon a fixed starre, and not a mobile or uauering planette, I coulde not (I must confesse) haue thocht my selfe fullie secure of a thankefull meiting, quhill from youre selfe I hadde bene certified of youre thankefull acceptance of my lettir by a direct and dewtiefull ansoure thairunto, as laitlie ye haue done; but being (as I haue allreaddie said) well aquaintid uith youre qualities, and resolued that I delt with a uyse man, I no sooner uas certaine that my lettir uas putt in youre handis, but as soone I laide my counte euer after *dormire securus in utramque aurem* for youre pairt, and thairfore maye ye assure youre self that I doe accepte of youre most uyse and kynde ansoure as only proceeding from the feruentie of youre affection, quhiche hath made you to surmount all doubtis of incurring suche hazairdis thairby as one in youre place is euer subiect unto, accounting non youre honest affection so muche the more preciouse unto me that ye have neuer untymouslie and undeutifullie snatched at future fortunes, quhiche unlawfull forme of doing micht some daye tende as farre to my owin discontentement; protesting in the presence of god that, uith his grace, I shall euer keepe that alyke christiane as politike reule, to measure as I uould be measured unto, and since (god be praised) my claime is both iuste and honorable, euer to ioyne the aduerbe to the name in using *bonum bene.*

It is indeid trew, as in youre owin lettir ye confesse, that if youre sylence hadde continued any longer it micht haue bredde sum hazairdis to the fortunes of both the princes (besydes youre owin particulaire), for as princes must heare and see uith other cares and eyes then thaire owin, so (to deale plainlie uith you) it uas continuallie beatin in my caris that youre sylence did proceede, not of dewtie to youre souueraine, but out of unquenchable malice against me; for, althoch I thocht it euer the pairte of a uyse man to inge by certaine effectis, and not by outuarde and deceauable apperances, yett too many impressions micht in the ende haue proued it to be trew that *gutta cauat lapidem, non in sed sepe cadendo,* so as by youre breaking of sylence at this tyme ye haue not onlie reaped the full assurance of my constant fauoure, but also done most honest seruice to youre owin souueraine, by remouing suche iealousies as micht other uayes haue brangled oure amitie, quhiche, allthoch it be not conuenient that she know, (by reason of her iealousie,) yett is it most avowable hou soone it shall come to licht, promeising to you for my pairt, in the honoure of a king, that not only shall I neuer by any untymouse impatience preasse in the least iote to diuert you from youre dewtie-full fidelitie to youre souueraine, but shall also in all tymes cumming reule all my actions for aduauncing of my lawfull future hoapes by youre aduyce, euen as ye uaire one of my owin counsaillouris all-readdie, being justlie moued to this confidence in you, as uell by the experience of youre uisdome and sinceritie in her seruice, as by the uyse and honest aduyce ye giue me hou to behaue myself touardis her, in your laite most kynde and uyse lettir, assuring you that I will not only use youre honest aduyce in my behauioure touardis her, (as I proteste to god I was neuer other uayes enclyned,) but I uill also use and follou youre other aduyce concerning my behauioure uith her people.

No! ye ueid not to thinke that I ame so euill aquentid uith the histories of all aages and nations that I ame ignorant quhat a rottin reide *mobile uulgus* is to leane unto, since some in youre cuntrey haue uerrie derelie bocht the experience thairof of lait. I ame no usurper; it is for thaime to play the absalon. Yea, god is my uitnes that I shall euer eschew to giue the quene any iuste cause of iealousie, through my to bissie behauioure, and besydes that, I euer did holde this maxime, that a few great spirites uaire the ordinarie instrumentis and seconde causis that made the uorlde to be reuled according to thaire temperature; other uayes I behoued by fauouring democratic fichte against my self, but yett is it trew indeid that the hairtis of the people are not to be reieetid, but not to be compassid by any particulaire insinuation uith euerie one of thaime, quhiche uolde breide greatter iealousie in the quene then goode successe uith thaime; but goode gouuernement at home, firme amitie uith the quene, and a louing caire in all things that maye concerne the uell of that state, are the onlie three steppes quhairby I thinke to mounte upon the hairtis of the people; and suirlie I ame importunid by sindrie thaire more then I coulde uishe, for feare thay beuraye thaimsellis, for I coulde be uerrie well contentid to be sure of thaire goode uill uithout the renewing of many messages, and in speciall I coulde uishe the dittaye of "I saye nothing" micht haue a goode simpathie uith the owner thairof, as for my pairte I shall follow the aduyce of my faithfull 3 [Lord Henry Howard] thairin.

And thus, hauing unfoldit before you the anatomie of my mynde, I hairtlie praye you to rest assured that, althoch to mercenarie men I uolde keipe promeise for my owin respect, but uithout any care for thaire uell-doing, yett the only respecte that can moue you and my faithfull 3 [Lord Henry Howard] to loue me being for the loue of vertu, I shall euer aquyte it in that uertuouse sort that I shall neid no other remembrancer for you both then my inuarde gratitude to sturre me to be cairfull both for present reseruidnes and futoure fauouris in the owin tyme.

      Youre most louing freinde,
         30 [KING JAMES].

[*No address. The seal gone.*]
[*Indorsed by Sec. Cecil,*]
 30 to 10
  2d. lettre.

No. IV.

10 [SEC. CECIL] TO 30 [KING JAMES].

[HATFIELD MSS. VOL. CXXXV. FOL. 61. ORIG. DRAFT IN THE HANDWRITING OF SEC. CECIL.]

When I beheld this second lettre of yours, so full of wisedom, greatnes and moderation, it gaue my mynd a dobble consolation, first, becawse I fownd you vouchsafed to dispense with my borrowed hand, which broght you no colored merchandise, next, becawse it shewed plainly that whensoever men of honesty shall deale with your Majesty that they do still *in portu nauigare*.

In this contemplation of your disposition I took no long deliberation at first to make an answer to your embassadors sommons, becawse my integrity needed no counsaile how to limit my answers within the bounds of loialty; yet dyd I let them plainly see, that I was fully minded to vse such provydence in all my proceedings, as to observe and discover whyther your Majesties mynd (which had ben so long possessed with preiudice,) wold be satisfied sufficiently with just apologys, and by an afectionat profession only of my desires to do yow those humble services which stand precisely with reall duty to my soverain and convenient caution to my poor fortune, of both which tributes when you find any person careles in his professions, I beseech your Majesty to believe that of those blossoms you shall never reap other then blasted fruicts of trechery and folly. For, in the first, I hold it certain that he that is fals to the present will neuer be treu to the future, and, in the second, I see by experience that *contra fatales morbos nullum est remedium*.

How things do pass in this estate which haue any essentiall reference to your Majesties fortune it may please you to receaue from yowr worthy 3 [Lord Henry Howard], whom I do informe of all things necessary, there being nothing more vnfitt, nor more vnsafe, then often wryting vppon needles grounds; for, syr, as in any case which necessarily requires advertisement or prevention, the meanest man that liveth shall be no more prodigall of his labour then I will, so when I do know that there is nothing which concerns you to purpose (or if there be some idle thing, that it shall prove to [be] nothing) I will take such freedom then, out of myne owne sincerity, and* from the trust which you please to promise me, as not to play the nouellant in steed of the watchfull centinell, so farr, I say, the centinell as if in matter of succession any base spiritts shall sett any practise on foot, I will not only advertise it, thogh it be but *in embrione*, but if it shall, in any counsaile or convention, great or small, publick or privat, come to voice or question, I will shew myself in an honest and resolute opposition as farr as tong or power is able. *Sed quorsum perditio hæc, cum ex nihilo nihil fit?* For I beseech your majesty giue me the honour thus farr to belieue me, that shold not be a stranger to all things of such nature which can occurr in this estate, that, First, the subiect it self is so perilous to toutch amongst vs, as it setteth a mark vppon his hedd for ever that hatcheth such a byrd†; next, on the fayth I ow to God, that there is neuer a prince or state in Europ with whom either mediate or imediate her Majesty hath entred into speach these xij. yeares of that subiect. No! as it is trew that, such is our misfortune, as it in her Majesties mind a capitall thing to settle, so is it not in her hart so much as to bethink her how to divert it, and therefore, if yow will distinguish between the pamphlets and proiects of priests and fugitiues, who are alwaies labouring to sett up one golden calf or other, as their fortune or fancy leadeth them, and the negotiations between princes or their ministers, retaining such a belief in some well chosen professions, as neyther to be ielous of sylence because you hear other idle eechos, nor mistrustfull of care and industry because every thing we do is not howerly made demonstratiue to yow, then may I, and all as I, say to them selfs securely, that they haue found in you a hart of adamant in a world of feathers.

* "the" stands in the draft after "and," which has been obviously left standing by mistake in the course of some alterations. It was originally intended to write "and the confident trust."

† "an egg" was first written, and in striking it out great part of the "egg" was left standing.

Lastly, renoumed prince, where you voutchsafe to shew me, that you will vse no other stepps for your gradation to assure the right you haue to your future fortune but a constant care to conserve the the queens good will entierly, to retaine the affections of her honest subiects, and to invite them to respect you by shewing them an example of your kingly government, I haue little more to say, besydes that comfort I take to see the mynd which I do reverence so well tempered, but that when all the roots and fractions of nombers shalbe serched by the greatest mathematicks you will fynd that this is only the golden nomber which will shew you *veram Galaxiam*, for all other plotts are dreames, and all other counsails such as Almighty God will scatter lyke chaff from of the earth; to whose blessed protection of yow in your religious and just resolutions I do comend you in my devotions, and ever remaine in humblest afections after one, and her alone, at your Majesties comandment, humbly and honestly,†

R. C.

[*Indorsed by Sec. Cecil,*]
4 Octobris, 1601.
2 Lettre,
10 to 30.

---

* The successive changes made by Cecil before he finally fixed upon this conclusion are worthy of note. Doubt arose in his mind after he had written the words " ever remaine." His first intention was to proceed with the sentence in some contemplated form of which " my sover " was written, and then struck out. The second thought was to follow " remain " with "after Cæsar, yours above all." The third attempt was by insertion of the words " to command " between " yours " and "above all, R. C." In the fourth, every thing after " remain " was struck out, and the termination made to stand " Yours affectionately and humbly, Ro. CECYLL." The fifth change ended in the adoption of the words as they now stand, but these were not approved without some erasures, and the insertion of the word " in " twice before " humblest afections," both at the end and the beginning of a line. So it still stands.

No. V.

30 [KING JAMES] TO 10 [SIR ROBERT CECIL].

[HATFIELD MSS. VOL. CXXXV. FOL. 63. ORIG. AUTOGRAPH.]

Mistake not, I praye you, my dearest 10 [Sir Robert Cecil], the honest sinccaritie of my meaning, in kaice I seame by this paper some quhat to uarie from these groundis and transcende these limites quhiche first uaire promeised and agreed upon betuixt us, in drawing on a more affectionatlie familiare, thoch lawfull, correspondence betuixt us, then uas at oure first dealing promeised by me to be urged, or by you to be parformed: but ye maye, notuithstanding heirof, boldlie repose in that securitie of his upricht and honorable intention that deales uith you, that, althoch sindrie interuenining accidents maye in sum sort chainge my style of uryting, yett shall I neuer in substance uarie one iote from these maine pointes quhiche at oure first aquaintance I did promise, and nowe unto you.

For I must plainlie confesse that both ye and youre faithfull collegue 40 * haue by youre uigilant and iudiciouse caire, so ayselie settelid me in the only richt course for my goode, so happelie preseruid the quenis mynde from the poison of icalouse præiudice, so ualiantlie resisted the crooked coursis of sum seditiouse spirits quho can neuer uearie seacretlie to sting the heiles of honest men, quhom thay onlie enuye for uertues sake, and so carefullie labourid to furder all my reasonable and lawfull endis, as the great proofe I haue hadd of your happie and honest concurrance for my uell doth force me, out of the abondance of a thankefull mynde, to uryte in a more louing, plaine, and familiare style then euer I was uoonte to doe before.

But not that heirby I have any intention to desyre you or 40 (quhom I alluayes and euer shall accounte as one) any uayes to alter, ather in forme or substance, youre accustumed forme of ansouring me, for, althoch that I, in respect of my birth and place, can not fall under the censure of any daingerouse constructions (thoch I neuer

---

* The person indicated by 40 has not been discovered.

uith goddis grace shall doe any thing in priuate quiche I maye not uithout shame proclaime upon the toppes of housis), yett so daingerouse is youre state, as subjectis, that althoch youre intention to youre souueraigne be neuer so upricht, yett, if the lyon thinke youre cares to be hornes thaire uill be no place admitted you for excuse: it shall thairfore suffise me that ye rest in a full and certaine persuasion of my loue and thankefull mynde to you both, quhairof this my hand urytte shall serue for a witnesse unto you, assuring 40 that, uith goddis grace, he shall neuer be disappointed of his confidence in my honestie upon youre relation, and as it neuer uas, nor shall be, my course to preasse him, or any, beyonde the boundis of thaire dewtifull allegeance to thaire souueraine, so doe I protest in goddis presence that, if I hadd uronged any of you so farre as to haue suspectid you guiltie of so great unuorthinesse, I uolde not haue so farr stained my conscience, and honoure, as to haue fosterid so uyle a motion, not for the gaining of the quhole worldis monarchie unto me.

I can not also omitte to displaye unto you the great contentement I receaue by youre so inuarde and united concurrence in all the pathes that leade to my future happinesse, most hairtelie uishing you to continew in that happie course as ye maye be sure of my thankefulnes touardis you, quhom I know to be only moued for the respect of conscience and honoure, to deserue so uell at the handis of a lawfull, naturall and louing successoure to youre quene and cuntrey; and thus praying 40 to be assured that by youre meanes only he shall heare from me, that he maye thairby discerne if any other uorde come to him in my name that it is but false and adulterate coine, and persuaiding him of my enteare affection touardis him, as to youre self, I bidde you hairtelie fairuell

Youre most assured louing freinde,
30 [KING JAMES.]

From falkelande the thridde of iuine, 1602.

[*Addressed by King James,*] " 10."

[Fastened in two places with crimson silk, and sealed also in two places, with a seal bearing a saltire, or St. Andrew's cross, on an escutcheon.]

No. VI.

10 [SIR ROBERT CECIL] TO 30 [KING JAMES].

[HATFIELD MSS. VOL. CXXXV. FOL. 65. ORIG. DRAFT IN THE HANDWRITING OF SEC. CECIL.]

Althogh the wisedome and sincerity of fidel 3 [Lord Henry Howard] do clearly represent the dayly circumstances of all particulers which do concern you, yet when I do behold your extraordinary favour in vouchsafing me the honour of your owne princely lettres, I can not quiet the affections of mine owne mynd, if I shall injoine them alwayes to speake *in tertia persona*. I beseech your Majesty, therfore, (after receauing my humble thanks for yowr so gracious acceptance of my poor indevours whilst the Duke was here,) to believe thus much, that the sight of yowr last dispatch dyd breed in me two powerfull passions:—the first of ioy and admiration of your roiall integrity and temper, whom I do still observe so free from desire of any mans afection, further then *suum cuique tribuere, et alterum non lædere*, as any honest man may so cary hym self* in all things towards yow, as if it shold happen that the vaile of secresy were taken of by errour or by destiny, the Quene her self (who were likest to resort to ielousy) shold (notwithstanding) still discern clearly, that whatsoever hath passed in this correspondency hath wholy tended to her owne repose and safety, without any incrochment vppon other lyberty then swch as divers good phisitiens do take when they deceaue an indisposed patient by giving *salutaria pro soporiferis*.

The second perturbation I must confess was only owt of dowbt and feare, lest the treasure of such a princes secret trust coming to light, either by the levity of those that haue offerd trafick, or by their owne election of loose instruments, might call in question my

---

* This was originally written "so to cary them selfs;" in the process of alteration "them" was altered into "hym," but the final letter of "selfs" was omitted to be struck out. I have made this obvious correction in the text.

gratitude for such a favour, or my sincerity in making vse of such a confidence, (especially when I am so acquainted with some of their vnsecresys,) as vppon evry flux of humour the secretest arctery of their hart is like the sive of Danae that leaked faster then the springs cold fill it, which she frequented howerly.

In which consyderation, renowmed prince, (be it spoken without deminution of my impressions of yowr roiall fauours,) althogh it is most trew that by my knoledg of particulers from you I shalbe better able to convert all such merchandise to yowr advantadge, yet, rather then the creditt of my sincerity shold be in danger to be tainted by any accident (beyond my power to remedy), I wold most humbly crave it of your Majesty that I might rather be left to mine owne discouerys of their greatest secretts, then to receaue any lyght from you of their deepest misteryes. For this I do profess in the presence of Him that knoweth and searcheth all mens harts, that if I dyd not some tyme cast a stone into the mouth of these gaping crabbs, when they are in their prodigall humour of discourses, they wold not stick to confess dayly how contrary it is to their nature to resolue to be vnder your soverainty; thogh they confess (Ralegh especially) that (*rebus sic stantibus*) naturall pollicy forceth them to keep on foot such a trade against the great day of mart. In all which light and soddain humours of his, thogh I do no way check him, becawse he shall not think I reiect his freedome or his affection, but alwaies (*sub sigillo confessionis*) vse contestation with him, that I neyther had nor ever wold *in individuo* contemplate future idea, nor ever hoped for more then iustice in time of change, yet, vnder pretext of extraordinary care of his well doing, I have seemed to disswade him from ingaging him self to farr, even for him self, much more therfore to forbeare to assume for me, or my present intentions.

Let me therfore presume thus farr vppon your Majesties favour, that whatsoever he shall take vppon him to say for me, vppon any new humor of kyndness, wherof sometyme he wilbe replete (vppon the receipt of privat benefite), you will no more believe it (if it come in other shape), be it neuer so much in my comendation, then

that his owne conscience thoght it needfull for him to vndertake to
keep me from any humour of imanity, when, I thank God, my
greatest adversaries and my owne sowle haue euer acquited me from
that of all other vices. Wold God I were as free from ofense
towards God, in seeking for privat affection to support a person
whom most religious men do hold anathema.

But why do I thus farr presume to troble your cares so much
with my poor privat griefs at his ingratitude to me, when I resolued
rather to record my privat ioies? I will therfore leave the best and
worst of him, and other things, to 3 [Lord Henry Howard's] relation, in whose discretion and affection you may *dormire securus;*
but this I will beseech, that, however your Majesty shall resolue *in
omnem euentum* to serve your self of their professions, whom the
D[uke] conceaueth to have gaigned as so fitt instruments for you, that
you will thus farr please to give me creditt as to beliove that, whensoever yow shall (without great occasion, palpably seen to the world)
imploy a person of any so eminent qwality, whose experience is no
better (thogh otherwise he be very worthy) in distinguishing
between ventosity and verity, he will leaue more clay and rubbish
behynd him in our streets then some of the best labourers you haue
can be able to cleanse in seven yeares after. For it is to well knowen
to me that during his aboad (what with the discourses of his followers and the noyse that he had great resort vnto him, the changing
of his lodging, the refusing to see (one tyme) the Queens phisitien,)
that such ielousy was raised of his bestowing his time in privat conferences and accesses, as, althogh her Majesties mind was well
prepared towards you before hand (with long foresight), yet was it
one of our greatest industryes euen to effect any reasonable desires,
without suspicion of some privat end or inward afection. Where,
on the other syde, it may be noted that, notwithstanding both your
former Ministers arrivall here in a time when my soverains hart was
bytterly inflamed with preiudice against your self and them, yet by
their great discretion and observation they conducted all their sowre
business to so good endes, and handled her so well, and evry other,

as that when they took their leaue there was no more remain of any ill impressions then is of the flights which byrds do make in th'ayre; to which I must also add, that in the manadging of all this correspondency I receave so good assurance by proofs infallible, to which neyther your Majesty nor they are privy, as I am no way curious, you see, in all things confidently *liberare animam meam.*

I will therfore conclude with this petition, that whensoever I shall take vppon me most to perswade you, either one way or other, to that which shalbe contrary to the prudent rules of your owne great iudgment, it will please you onely to suffer my good meaning to pleade my pardon; so shall you be assured that on the earth he treads not that is or shalbe (next my dearest vowes to my soverain) more humbly or afectionatly ready to do you service then is your Majesties for ever assuredly.

Addressed: " 10 to 30."

Sealed with three impressions in red wax of a circular seal bearing a lion rampant.

Indorsed in Cecil's hand " Febrr."

No. VII.

10 [SIR ROBERT CECIL] TO 30 [KING JAMES].

[HATFIELD MSS. VOL. CXXXV. FOL. 67. DRAFT, NOT IN CECIL'S HAND, BUT CORRECTED BY HIM.]

May it please your Majesty,

When I reade over most of those dispatches (after they are written) which 10 [Sir Robert Cecil] and 3 [Lord Henry Howard] doe soe often send you, I confesse I should for many considerations change countenance at my owne errours, if I had not now sufficiently beheld your vertues in their trewest colours. For what could be more absurd for men of common sense then still to pester a prince (whose tyme is precious) with so many pety particulers, if we had not tryed your habite of pacience; and what ought men of any understandinge to be more afrayd of then to offer soe much counsell to a prince of soe much understandinge, if it weare not trew that we haue founde in your mynde a plentifull springe of favour and gratitude. For in my owne particuler, when I doe wey my actions in indifferent balance, I am soe farr from assumption of any extraordinary desert, as I assure your Majesty I scarcely picke vpp graynes inough to make vpp half an ounce of valuable meritt, and therefore must only hope that ether you will, with the civillians, *reputare voluntatem pro facto*, or imitate the Godes (whose image you [carry*]) and soe *creare ex nihilo*.

For the matter, therefore, which I doe offer to your consideration, it is, that you will be pleased to write to my Souverayne to that effect which followeth, wherein, as I will leave to discourse of all the motives of my desyre to haue you write, to the faythfull pen of your affectionate 3 [Lord Henry Howard], which shall deliver you *principium et finem*, soe doe I whoaly and absolutely leaue the matter to your owne wisedome, and my proposition to your gracious interpretation. Butt I must here deliver (in my owne proper sence) because my hart speakes it, that if your Majesty (for your owne particuler service) shall not thinke it fitt that I doe still (according to the proper institution of my place) give eare to Iew and Gentile, I will change myne owne custome, and abridge my owne priveledge, with your owne subieetes, rather then to be putt every hower to the racke of my owne wittes, to prevent that mischeife which I should think to haue done my self, if in any action I should but incurre the least suspicone, howsoever you should receave any after satisfaccone. As for any other rumours or fond discourses of idle braynes, I know it is so impossible for men (in my place) to avoyd them (seeinge I must heare discontented sprittes, imploy men *male fidei*, and reward men for particulers whoe are otherwise vnsounde *in radice*), as I referre all

---

* The original stood "you you carry." In striking out the second "you" the corrector's pen ran on and erased also the succeeding word. I have inserted it, as necessary to the sense.

to Godes providence, and serve my prince and countrey with ioy and confidence; and yet because contynuall practise and envy at hoome and abroade may rayse soe many probable arguments, as if I doe contynew dayly by my lettres to preoccupate or confute them, such will be the frequencye of my dispatches, as it cannot be free from iealous observation.

In this respect I haue heretofore presumed to doe two thinges; first, to move you to write to the Queen (because her woordes may be as quiett as her actions), for they movinge oft vppon such reportes as flye abroade (which never soe abounded as now) that greater freedome is yeilded to all your subiectes that travayle through this countrey (and spare not to discourse at random), are often sharpe to strangers, as well as to those about her, though otherwise, to preiudice you or yours in any matter of importance, be pleased to take my trew and purest vowes and protestations that she is as free from it as your Majesties owne hart could wyshe.

The next thinge which I did now thinke fitt to recommend to your consideration was, to acquaynt you with the causes which make me hold intelligence with Gray, because I am infinitely desyrous to be able to say (vppon your answeare and dyrection which I will follow), *Anima, quiesce.* Beseechinge your Majesty (howsoever you give me liberty to write often or seldome) to beleive that I am soe farr, and wilbe, from any reservation or remissnes to advertise you (when I fynde any thinge to concerne you in honour or safetye) as if there should happen in one night an vniversall deluge of all the posts of England, I would make the only soonn of my body serve for a postilian, to carry my packett, before the least haire of your head should miscarrye which yow could not spare. And as it is trew that your constant advised and vninfected flocke, greater, I assure your Majesty, now then my pen shall need to expresse, in power and place, are so devoted to the present, as all the earth cannot change their duty or devide their affections from her person, to whom their only allegeance is dew (vntill allmighty God shall otherwise dispose of her), soe vouchsafe me in this to be your oracle, that when that day (soe greivous to us) shall happen which is the tribute of all mortall creatures, your shippe shalbe steered into the right harbour, without crosse of wave or tyde that shalbe able to turne over a cockboate, for which many that will talke now, and brave it, wilbe fitter pilotts then yet they can be; for, Sir, soe idle and soe superfluous are many of the double dilligences which divers humours would insynuate, because they want power and knowleidge in the mysterye of this government, and of the Queenes disposition, as if, vuknown to them,* many of their errours weare not palliated, they wold loose you that which is and wilbe your greatest safe[t]y, though it may try your patience.† For God doth know I speake truth, that her vnwonted forme of seeinge and vsinge all your subiectes now, with extraordinary courtesyes to them towardes her, if you recommend them, makes the myndes of those that otherwise haue noe affection, but rather secrett indisposition, to you and your nation, privately conclude that you are written her successour *in corde*, though not *in ore aperto*. This course of hers is that which diverteth and prepareth and bindeth all mens harts, which otherwise would stand at gase, and like trew worldlinges only goe and come accordinge to occasion. And soe I humbly take my leaue, with prayers to God that he will send both you and yours eternall blessinges.

At your Majestys commandment
humbly and absolutely, my duty
first reserved.

Indorsed, Copye to the King.

---

* In the original draft here were inserted the following words in a parenthesis: " for God forbidd they knew me, how much soever they have been bound to me."

† Instead of the passage " they wold loose .... try your patience," there originally was written the following : " I doe protest to your Majesty insteed of their fonde and gyddie offeringe you themselfes (whose power and vertue beeinge tryed will spend in fume) they would loose you the Queen, whose mynde keapt secure and kynd you have found the trew Philosopher's stone ! "

No. VIII.

30 [KING JAMES] TO 10 [SIR ROBERT CECIL].

[HATFIELD MSS. VOL. CXXXV. FOL. 69. ORIG. AUTOGRAPH.]

My deerest and trustie 10 [Sir Robert Cecil,] My penne is not able to expresse hou happie I thinke my self for hauing chauncid upon so uorthie, so uyse, and so prouident a freinde as 10 [Sir Robert Cecil] is, quhiche ye coulde not bettir haue manifestid then by that honest aduyce ye giue me for uritting to xxiiii. [Queen Elizabeth], and althoch I haue uerrie lately urytten unto her some quhat concerning that subiect, yett haue I now againe uritten this other, according to youre aduyce, onely this farre I wishe you to be aquaintid with, that in treuth suche remon[s]trances as ye sent me uaire neuer presentid unto me, and as for the frenshe ambassadoure, he hath often upon his oathe purged him self unto me that he hath no direction to moue any suche matter; for it uas muche noised amongst oure ministerie that his only carande to Skotlande uas to craue libertie of conscience, and thairfore I had no uill to putte my self in use of lyeing, but as indeid I uas laitely aduertished by some subiectis of my owin out of france that great offers uaire to be sent me from spayne, and that upon condition of graunting liberty of conscience, so did I treuly aduertishe the quene thairof, as uell in my laste as in this, quhairin I haue follouid youre groundis, only leauing out some phrasis that in my opinion smellid of* flatterie, and some others that seemed too shairpe, and to accuse her of mistrusting me.

Alluayes, quhen ye haue redde the coppie of my letre, I leaue it to youre discretion, quho best knowis her humoure, quhither to presente it or not, quhairin I must repose upon youre discreit fidelitie, that if it maye please her and uorke goode effectis, it maye be putte in her handis, other uayes that ye maye freelie aduertishe me quhat ye uolde haue to be mendit thairin.

As for youre course in tyme cumming with the maister of graye,

---

* Two words concealed here, by having been written over, apparently not by the writer.

I remitte my opinion thairin to 20 [the Earl of Mar] his lettir, but this farre I hairtely praye you to assure youre self, that ye can haue no dealing with quhatsumeuir, iewe, gentile, or heathen, that euer uill breede the least suspition in me, of any crakke in youre integritie touardis me, but by the contraire the further ye are upon thaire secreates the more able uill I be to sitte as a godd upon all the imaginations of thaire hairtes, and the more secure uill my state be from all thaire practises, quhairof ye haue allreadie giuen me so lairge a proofe, that if euer I needit any moe apologies or excuses in that maitter I uaire not worthie of the place I posesse, nay, by the contraire, ye maye assure youre self that I truste no more in the fidelitie of 20 [the Earl of Mar] that of a chylde was brocht up with me,* then I doe in you, protesting that thir uordis doe only proceede *ex abundantia cordis*, and not of any intention to paye you with italiane complementoes, and thairfore I doe quhollie remitte it to youre owin discretion, and as ye shall fynde the necessitie of tyme to requyre it, to use greatter or lesse frequentie of advertishementis; and thus uith my most hairtie comendations to my deare and faithfull 3 [Lord Henry Howard] I bidde you hairtelie fare uell.

      Youre constantly assured freind
          30 [KING JAMES.]

[*Addressed, probably not by King James,*]
  "3."

Sealed in two places with a seal impressed on red wax, bearing three piles issuing from a chief, with a roundel on each, and on the chief a crescent. On the dexter side of the shield is the letter G., and there are traces of a letter, perhaps M, above the shield; the letter on the sinister side has not caught the impression.

[*Indorsed by Sir Robert Cecil,*]
  "30 to 10."

---

* Nearly a line, consisting of fourteen or fifteen words, has here been concealed by having been scribbled over.

IX.

30 [KING JAMES] TO 10 [SIR ROBERT CECIL].

[HATFIELD MSS. VOL. CXXXV. FOL. 71. ORIG. AUTOGRAPH.]

My dearest 10 [Sir Robert Cecil], I ame ashamed that I can as yett by no other meanes uitnesse my thankefulnes for youre daylie so honorable iudiciouse and painfull labouris for the furtherance of my greatest hoapes, then by baire inke and paper, and that youre trauellis of so great uorthe and inæstimable ualew shoulde be repayed uith so poore a recompence, but the best excuse is that these paperis are but uitnessis of that treasure of gratitude quhiche by youre goode desairtis is daylie noorished in my hairte.

I ame not a lytle encouraged by the letre of 24 [Queen Elizabeth] quhiche discoveris a great integritie in her affection, and plainnes in her dealing; quhom I oucht to thanke for her goode temper, ye may easilie guesse. I haue ansourid her in the best sorte I coulde, as by the coppie thairof ye will persaue, and that ye maye haue proofe that my confidence is fullie setlid upon you, I haue sent you the substance of tuo messages that Sir Antonie Shurley hath latelie sent me, uithout keeping up one iote thairof, quhose errouris appeare rather to proceide from ignorance then malice. Ye can not doe me a greatter seruice then to moue 24 [Queen Elizabeth] to continew this inuarde and privie forme of intelligence, quhairby I hoape ye shall in the ende proue a honest and happie minister.

To faithfull 8 [Mr. Edward Bruce] his lettir I remitte all particulairs, and speciallie my opinion hou ye shall behaue youre self in that maitter, quhiche, god knowis, is more greeuouse unto me then any temptation that satan by goddis permission coulde haue deuysed to haue aflicted me uith. But heir I ende, with the assurance of the continuance of my constant loue to my most faithfull 3 [Lord Henry Howard], assuring him that, as I ame infinitelie sorie for that defluxion fallin upon his eye, so uoulde I thinke ane hospitall a reuairde that uolde keepe no proportion, ather for a kings honoure to giue, or by him for so uell meriting seruices to be receaued. And thus, my dearest 10 [Sir Robert Cecil], I bidde both you and 3 [Lord Henry Howard] most hairtelie fair uell.

Your moste louing and assurid freind

30 [KING JAMES].

[Addressed,]

"30 to 10."

Fastened in two places with crimson silk, and sealed with two impressions of a seal bearing, a saltire, on a chief three crowns, and above the letter M, with E on the dexter side and B on the sinister; probably intended to designate "Mr. Edward Bruce."

[Indorsed by Sir Robert Cecil,]

"30 to 10, concerning the Queen."

No. X.

10 [SIR ROBERT CECIL] TO 30 [KING JAMES].

[HATFIELD MSS. VOL. CXXXV. FOL. 72. DRAFT IN THE HANDWRITING OF SIR ROBERT CECIL.]

It is the property of the creator to accept the labours of men according to his knoledg of their desire withowt measure of their ability. Of this devine qwality, if ever mans eys beheld on earth a lively image, the same appearith in your person, from whom I haue receaued so iust a censure and so gracious an acceptation of my proceedings. Let therfore this petition in this lettre craue at once from you two severall pardons; th' one for me, th' other for it self. For me, that I haue no sooner sent the humble acknowledgment of your favour, which I had not failed to do, if respects to yowr owne service had not staied the dispatch; for it self, in that (being admitted an imediat messinger to so complete a prince) it delivereth not all which it hath in chardg, a fawlt swerly vnpardonable, if any paper or any woords cold containe it, but your Majesties exqvisite judgment can not but know, that that which I can tender you, must be finite, imperfect, and of small valew, thogh the dwty, the affection and zealous thankfulness of my hart be like your favors, infinite, perfect, and matchless.

For that which may concern the branded sheep, be pleased to secure your self of these two things;—first, that here is so little disposition to do fauour, as there is more question whyther sylence shall not be the answer to those with whom (for their qwality and many other good respects) I cold rather wish more decorum observed. Next (which were impiety in me to conceale) that in the recomendation, there appeared no shew of other affection then that which may proceed meerly from the abused pity *d'un bon nature*, and therfore how much so ever Grey his relations, with his coments and paraphrases, corrupt evry text whereon he readeth, eyther there or here, I beseech your Majesty to assure your self that althogh I have ben oft constrained, (for prevention of suspicion in his multiplying braine) to couer my affection, (sometyme with the vaile of dispaire, sometyme with the mislike of open carriadge of all addresses,) that God hath neuer so farr forsaken me, as to suffer me to leaue it in the power of swch a vyper to tax me by woord or writt of malicious practise, intention of preiudice, or so much as a desire to procure the good of this state *in substantivo* by an euill adverb. For your answer likewise sett downe for me, your Majesty shall find, God willing, that as I haue hytherto ben farr from any contrary course, hauing alwaies observed that the practises of both kingdoms ar principally grounded uppon the contemplation of her Majesties disposition to mislike or approve them, so there cold neuer haue come to me a more joyfull direction, then when I perceaved that by observing yowr owne iudiciall comandments, sett downe in 8 [Mr. Edward Bruce] his lettre, I shold obey both yow and mine owne conscience.

Lastly, for that which your Majesty saw of my hand writing, my purpose is not non to iniury [*sic*] your princely constancy with idle apologies, which wold sauour of folly and weaknes, only I wold be gladd to impart to your Majesty some circumstances, becawse you may be able to iudg whyther that were counterfait or originall. Not long since this Thraso moved me to write some tyme vnto him in swch a manner as might secure you of his integrity, which cold be by no other meane so direct (he sayd) as if I wold write some lettres in swch sort as he might venter to bring them to you vnopened; hereby, sayth he, it will confirme that I am valued, if you continew correspondency, and it shall wype away the Kings ielousy if I adventure such an imediat delivery. In this he directed two principall grounds for my lettre, one that I wold make it appeare that he had comended the Marquis Huntly, for that wold please your Majesty and serve his tourn, to whom he fownd the Marquis a freend; thother, that I wold write that the Duke was wronged, to be charged with concealing of my lettre, when it was trew that Hambleton had it not, at first departure, but was sent after him. Of this subject was his desire to haue my lettre consist, which he wold shew, as owt of integrity, reserving other matter to my more privat lettre, which shold concern his other idle toyes and proiects. In this kind I dyd resolue to comply with him, for the most because I knew what foundation I had layd in your Majesties mind, but in that poinct of the Duke I varied a little from his compass, and writt only in the generall of him, becawse I knew not what present advantadg he might haue made of that part, which was so contradictory to treuth, and to thintent he shold see by my writing in that (which he ment to shew you) that I was farr from correspondency with your Majesty, I added further some what in that sense with the rest. If therfore he dyd shew you no other matter, then is sett downe by 8 [Mr. Edward Bruce] from your memory, it was the originall, wherin I see your Majesty need borrow no writing tables, for I assure you it was *in verbis conceptis*.

To conclude, thogh I do confess that his iniquitys towards me are such as flesh and blood cold hardly beare, yet God hath given me so much feeling of mine owne ofenses towards himself, as it racketh but breaketh not my charity; and for the rest, were it the greatest labour or sorrow, paine or perill, I shold despise them all to prevent yowr preiudice, to whom I will only presume to say this much, at this time;—first, that as it is a fawlt in any man to be so full of apprehensions as *nubem sumere pro Iunone*, so it hath ben the saying of the best nauigators, that a good master of a shypp shall lack many a tryfle in a storme which others will not esteem worthe taking vp in a calme; secondly, that whensoever so audacious thoghts hath seised the harts of subiects in a monarchy, to be workers of reformation, there enters also a constant resolution to extinguish all soverain power that may after censure their owne actions, *sed hoc non opus.* It is fitter for me to conclude with this, that when I behold the discreet and kynd conduct of this poor correspondency between your worthy 20 [Earl of Mar] and 8 [Mr. Edward Bruce] and us, I can not but in that one circumstance often acknoledg your happines, for whom God hath ordained ministers of so great wisedom and reservednes, with whose meritt towardis you, thogh I can not participate in their condition, yet I will pray for your safety when I can not watch over it, for your greatnes thogh I can add nothing to it, and confess that if I cold do more then any one, it were less then nothing (balanced with my desires), or if I cold do as much as all the world, it were farr inferiour to your vertew and gratitude.

[*Indorsed by Sir Robert Cecil,*]
 "A lettre to 30 in January."

No. XI.

30 [KING JAMES] TO 10 [SIR ROBERT CECIL].

[HATFIELD MSS. VOL. CXXXV. FOL. 76. ORIG. AUTOGRAPH.]

My dearest 10 [Sir Robert Cecil], In regairde that my trustie 3 [Lord Henry Howard], in a letre of his to 8 [Mr. Edward Bruce], wisheth him in youre name to make me aquainted of the laite uakening up againe of a commouning for a treatie of peace betwixt englande and spaine, craving my aduyce hou to behaue youre self thairin, I haue taken occasion by these few lynes, first, most hairtely to thanke you for youre tymouse aduertishement heirof, and nexte to sette you doune, as shortly as I can, my opinion thairanents. Quhen I haue aduysedlie considderit and deepelie looked in this maitter, I can not surelie but thinke that, the tyme being ueyed, and the present state of things, suche a peace at this tyme must be greatlie præiudiciall, first to the state of religion in generall, secondlie to the state, both in religion and policie of this yle in speciall, and lastlie most perrelouse for my iust claime in particulaire. Amongst many, three principall gatis for procuring these fore namid mischeifis by this peace uoulde appearantly be oppenid, first, *liberum commercium* betuixt these nations uolde so soundlie conciliate and extinguishe all former rankouris as it uolde no more be thocht odiouse for ane englisheman to dispute upon a spanishe tytle; secondlie, the king of spaine woulde thairby haue occasion, by his agents of all sortis, loadenit with golden argumentis, quho (if so uaire) uoulde haue free accesse in englande, to corrupte the myndes of all corruptible men for the aduancement of his ambitiouse and most iniuste pretencis, besydes the setling sure meanis for intelligence at all occasions; and lastly, iesuites, seminarie preistis, and that rable, quhair with englande is all readdie toe muche infectid, uoulde then resorte thaire in suche suarmes as the katerpillers or flyes did in ægipte, no man any more ahhorring thaime, since the spanishe practises uas the greatest cryme that euer thay uaire attaintid of, quhiche nou by this peace uill utterly be forgottin.

And nou, since I ame upon this subiecte, lette the proofes ye haue hadde of my louing confidence in you pleade for ane excuse to my plainnes, if I freelie shouue you that I greatlie uonder from quhence it can proceede that not only so great flokkis of iesuites and preistis darre both resorte and remaine in englande, but so proudlie doe use thaire functions throuch all the pairtis of englande uithout any controllement or punishement these dyuers yearis past; it is trew that for remedie thairof thaire is a proclamation lately sette furthe, but blame me not for longing to heare of the exemplaire execution thairof, *ne sit lex mortua*. I know it maye be iustlie thocht that I haue the lyke beame in my owne eye, but alace it is a farre more barbarouse and stiffe nekkit people that I rule ouer. Saint george surelie rydes upon a touardlie rydding horse, quhaire I ame daylie burstin in daunting a wylde unrculie coalte, and I proteste in goddis presence the daylie increase that I heare of poperie in englande, and the proude uanterie that the papistes makis daylie thaire of thaire powaire, thaire increase, and thaire combyned faction, that none shall enter to be king thaire but by thaire permission; this thaire bragging, I saye, is the cause that moues me, in the zeale of my religion, and in that naturall loue I owe to englande, to breake furthe in this digression, and to foreuarne you of these apparante euills; for thoch ye must know all these things farre bettir then I can, yet it is a trew olde saying, that ane other man will bettir see a mannis game then the player himself can doe. Thus maye ye see, my dearest 10 [Sir Robert Cecil], hou my loue to you hath bredde my plainness, for freindshippe uithout freedome is nothing but a fontaine of affectate complementis.

As to the state of things heir, I haue this long tyme past persaued a greate smoake, but as yett can neuer fynde out one sparke of the fyre, that I maye quenshe it, but I ame in hoape shortlie to discouer it, quhiche quhen I doe, I ame resoluid with handis and feete to treade it out soundlie; but the particulaire of this and all other things I remitte to 8 [Mr. Edward Bruce] his lettir, praying you to reste assurid that I shall neuer leaue of to deuyse how I shall some daye requyte the daylie great proofes that ye giue of youre affection touardis me, and in the meane tyme shall in my hairte constantlie remaine

Youre most louing and afectionate freinde,
30 [King James].

[*Indorsed by Sir Robert Cecil,*]
" 30 to 10; concerning Peace."

Fastened, in two places, with crimson silk, and sealed with two imperfect impressions of the seal of Mr. Edward Bruce already described at p. 27, with reference to letter No. IX.

No. XIII.

10 [SIR ROBERT CECIL] TO 30 [KING JAMES].

[HATFIELD MSS. NO. CXXXV. FOL. 78. DRAFT IN THE HANDWRITING OF SIR ROBERT CECIL, ENTITLED BY HIM

"MY LETTER IN ANSWER OF HIS MAJESTYS LETTER CONCERNING PAPISTS."]

The comfort which ariseth dayly in my hart out of your gracious proceeding with me drawes from me so lardg a measure of thankfulnes as woords and messingers wold faile, if I shold as often speake to that effect as I find cawse, or shold insist vppon particulers, which are infinite; I will therfore lern of Homer, that all springs owght to retourn to the ocean, from whence they took their being, and so, once for all, I acknoledg your owne vertews to be the only spring hedd of all my confidence.

That your Majesty vouchsafeth to acquaint me with the inward temper of your mynd, in matter of religion, I take for an vnspeakable fauour, for what can giue more rest to an honest man then to forsee the continued blessing of liuing under a religious Prince; and for my self, (if it be worthie your Majesties troble to take a reckning of so meane a mans privat conscience,) I will beseech you to know by this that I am in hope to concurr with Hierom, in this particuler, that *in qua fide puer natus sum, in eadem senex moriar*, so haue I ben bredd, so baptised, instructed, and lived. For the matter of priests, I will also cleerely deliuer your Majesty my mynd. I condemn their doctrine, I detest their conuersation, and I forsee the perill which the excersise of their function may bring to this iland, only I confess that I shrink to see them dy by dosens, when (at the last gasp) they come so neare loyalty, only becawse I remember that mine owne voice, amongst others, to the law (for their death) in Parliament, was ledd by no other principle then that they were absolute seducers of the people from temporall obedience, and confident perswaders to rebellion, and which is more, becawse that law had a retrospective to all priests made twenty yeares before. But contrariwise for that generation of vypars (the Iesuits), who make no more ordinary merchandise of any thing then of the blood and crownes of Princes, I am so farr from any compassion, as I rather look to receaue comandment from you to abstaine then prosecute. But of this matter there is inogh sayd, for, thogh I confess that neyther your comandment, nor the greatest power on earth, cold make me alter my pace, for privat consideration, in matter of blood, against my conscience (if it were otherwise then I tell yow), yet being, as I haue shewed it to be, as well against the priest as the iesuite, I will presume only for your Majestys satisfaction (against the preiudice of rumour) to let you know particulerly how her Majesty resolueth to proceed in this matter.

Their qwarrells are in print, and the cawses. They have *in diebus criticis* of the proclamation (wherof the last day limited is now expired) offred many declarations of that profession which they wold maintaine, hoping therby to procure some qwalification. Of this consyderation hath ben had, but we that are yowrs do so well know, first, that in this there is still imperfection and perill, and that they may haue dispensation to say much more then this; and, next, that howsoeuer they may pretend the vse of their function with distinctions and sophistry, that there can be no other effect then a toleration of idolatry (thogh mass be no treason), and a ready preparatif to the poysoned dyrection of Rome, as all is reiected, and no modyfication of the proclamation, but a lyberty now of their apprehension and execution; only to your Majesty in privat this I say, that in respect that some haue appealled to good purpose, and some haue don good services to the estate, and that their is much dyfferrence in mens spiritts, thogh not much in their crimes, it is resolued, that of those that are voluntaryly come in before the last date of the proclamation, there shalbe some charitable relief vsed to some of them, in prison or beyond seas, in which poinct, seing I find my boldnes not ill taken, I will affirme trewly to you, that most of them do declare their affection absolutly to your title, and some of them haue lernedly written of the validity of the same; a matter I towtch not as a motive to you to esteem them, for it wold be a horrour to my hart to imagin that they that are enemies to the gospell shold be held by yow worthy to be freends to your fortune, thogh the strength of that principle in succession teacheth all men to prevent (without synn) all manner of opposition. In which poinct if your Majesty saw [?] not the mystery of your owne wisedome, pardon me to dowbt, whyther yow shold now haue had cawse to deliberate how yow shold deale with the messinger from Antichrist.

For the peace, I hope your Majesty sees my cours (wold God no other dyd), for if I cold be tymorouse of the fortune which followes generall envy, God doth know it that as the coldnes of 40 in it now, for your only respect, hath lost him freends, so that scandall which followed the late Erl of Essex for his greedynes of warr, because he wold be euer sure of an army, is most transferred to me, as being an enemy for some other corrupt ends to the cours of pacification. But God (I thank him) hath to much blessed me from all the snares layd for me, to make my counsailes in government or matter of conscience subiect to the passions of feares and dowbts, who know full well that the sparrow lighteth not on the grownd *sine providentia Dei*.

And now to the last, which is of lest price (for so are all externall signes in regard of the internall affections);—the matter of the money I meane. Seing your Majesty hath pleased so princely to secure me that you have pardoned the presumption, I assure your Majesty there is to much sayd for your acceptation, for I plainly see that you are God's liuely image, that neuer measure the mynd by the valeu of the sacrifice, and therfore for the conueiance and order there is nothing now behynd for me but to deliuer the soomm yow send for to the hand that comes for it, and to beseech your Majesty that beyond the fygures of 20 [Earl of Mar] and 8 [Mr. Edward Bruce] this poinct may never be extended.

Toutching all other particulers I haue presumed by your fidel

3 [Lord Henry Howard], to shoot mine arrowes one after another, whom thogh I can not make either puritane or protestant, yet must I protest him to all men to be *et virum et ciuem bonum*, and towards your Majesty my lyfe shold be pledg, if it were needfull to you, that he hath ever ready his gantlet of defiance against Pope and Cardinalls in your qwarrell. Thus doth your Majesty see our naked harts, and in them all our errours, for which when our honest affection pleadeth at the barr of your roiall iudgment, what other advocate needeth but the benignity of that spiritt which ruleth all your counsailles and actions, wherin I beseech Almighty God to give yow happiest success, for so it is desired by him that is

Ever ready to do you all lawful and humble seruice.

No. XIV.

30 [KING JAMES] TO 10 [SIR ROBERT CECIL].

[HATFIELD MSS. NO. CXXXV. FOL. 80. ORIG. AUTOGRAPH.]

My dearest 10 [Sir Robert Cecil], The feare I haue to be mistaken by you in that pairt of my last lettir quhairin I discouer the desyre I haue to see the last edicte against iesuites and priestes putte in execution, the feare I saye of your misconstruing my meaning heirin (as appearis by youre ansoure), enforceth me in the uerrie throng of my greatest affaires to penne by poste ane ansoure and cleare resolution of my intention. I did euer hate alyke both extremities in any cace, only allowing the middes for uertue, as by my booke nou laitely published doeth plainly appeare. The lyke course doe I holde in this particulaire. I uill neuer allowe in my conscience that the bloode of any man shall be shedde for diuersitie of opinions in religion, but I uolde be sorie that catholikes shoulde so multiplie as thay micht be able to practise thaire olde principles upon us. I will neuer agree that any shoulde dye for erroure in faith against the first table, but I thinke thay shoulde not be permitted to comitte uorkes of rebellion against the seconde table. I uolde be sorie by the suorde to diminishe thaire nomber, but I uolde be also loathe that by soe great conniuence and ouer sicht geuin unto thaim thaire nomberis shoulde so encrease in that lande as by continuall multiplication thay micht at last becumme maisteris, hauing allreaddy suche a setled monarchie amongst thaime, as thaire archipreiste uith his tuelf apostles keeping thaire termis in Londone, and iudging all questions as uell ciuill as spirituall amongst all catholikes. It is for the præuenting of thaire multiplying, and new sett up empyre, that I longe to see the execution of the last edicte against thaime, not that thairby I uishe to haue thaire headis deuydit from thaire boddies, but that I uolde be glaidde to haue both thaire headdis and boddies separated from this quhole yland, and safely transported beyonde seas, quhaire thay maye freelie glutte thaime selfis upon thaire imaginated goddis. No! I ame so farre from any intention of persecution, as I·proteste to God I reuerence thaire churche as oure mother churche, althoch clogged uith many infirmities and corruptions, besydes that I did euer holde persecution as one of the infallible notes of a false churche. I only uishe that suche order micht be taken as the lande micht be purged of suche great flokkis of thaime that daylie diuertis the soulis of many from the sinccaritie of the gospell, and uithall that sum meanes micht be founde for debarring thaire entrie againe, at least in so great suarmes. And as for the distinction of thair rankis, I meane betuixt the iesuites and the seculaire preistes, althoch I denye not that the iesuites, lyke uenumid uaspes and fyre brandis of sedition, are farre more intollerable then the other sorte, that seame to professe loyaltie, yett is thaire so plausible profession the more to be distrusted that, lyke maried uemen or minors, quhose uowes are euer subiect to the controlment of thaire husbandis and tutoris, thaire consciences must euer be comandit and ouerreulid by thaire romishe god as it pleasis him to allowe or reuoke thaire conclusions. Thus, remitting all other matters to the lettirs of faithfull 8 [Mr. Edward Bruce], not being able to expresse my thankefulnes for youre so great care to furneishe a guairde unto me, and recomending me most hairtely to my most faithfull 40, I ende with renewing unto you the assurance of the constant loue of

Youre most louing freinde

30 [KING JAMES].

PART II.

CORRESPONDENCE WITH LORD HENRY HOWARD.

No. I.

8 [Mr. EDWARD BRUCE] TO 3 [LORD HENRY HOWARD].

[HATFIELD MSS. VOL. CXXXV. FOL. 81. ORIGINAL AUTOGRAPH.]

Vythin tuo dayes, deer and vorthy 3 [Lord Henry Howard], after my last sent unto yow, of the 3. of Auguste, come this packet to my hands, whiche i did carie wyth me to the hunting, where all was perused by 30 [King James], both wyth admiration and plesour. We did wonder greatly at your newes and no lese at the curiositie and diligence of 7 [Cobham*], that lewes no stounes wnstirred to make ws stwmble, and enterith at all oppennes wyth a rode in hes hand by charms to turne ws into serpents. It may be that suche bussie sperits trwble the watters of loue and fyll the springs of sownd frindshipp betuix 24 [Queen Elizabeth] and 30 [King James], yet can we not see in so dooing whow thay can fiche thair ends and desyrs; but we wer exceding well pleased to perceaue the grasse so finly cut under hes foots by that wery wise ansour whiche 10 [Sir

---

* This explanation is indicated in the original by the contemporary interlineation of "Cob." over the 7, and "Cobhā" written in the margin.

Robert Cecil] did make to 24 [Queen Elizabeth], wherein he did ouertake both 7 [Cobham's] to great heast and her to miche credulitie; but because time will detecte the treuthe of suche aduertisments, i will set yow doune simply what 30 [King James] knowes of this embassage.

My lord semple* at hes retourne from spaine did acquent the king that thair was euin propos thair to send ane embassadour in this contrie, and that it was contentuosly and muche dispute in thaire consell, *pro et contra*, some afferming that it was expedient to seeke the compeignes to be revoked by hes majestic wyche he hade sent to succour thair rebells in the low contries, vthers that thair king myht easily practise a diworse betuene the princes of this yle, if he would foster hes hopes, corrupt hes consell, and incourage hem wyth assurance to adwance hes title in the time of tryall and competion, and by thois means to weakin the holl yle and mak it a pray to thair conquis. To this opposition was made that the king of spaine could not in honor directe ane ambassadour to any prince befor he knewe whowe he sowld be receaued, spetially to hem whoo hade aidit and assisted hes naturall subiects to make warre agains hem in hes ouen dominions, agains the treaties of peas standing betuix the contries; that he was so far dewoted to yowr quene, and so manye stronge bands betuix thair contries, that it would proof impossible to diuerte hem frome her amitie; so, tossing thees doubts to and frome, thay broake up thair consell without any resolusion, attending, as he said, some greattar alienation of minds betuix our tuo princes, whiche before thay see i hope the best of thaire eyes sall be clossed eternally.

Since this time 30 [King James] protests that natheir directly nor indirectly he newer heard motion or speache of any suche message to come unto hem, and if it had bene so, he hade made her maiestic acquentid wyth it long or nowe. It may be, but it is not pro-

---

* Robert fourth Lord Semple, a Roman Catholic peer of Scotland, through whom King James communicated with the Court of Spain.

bable, that on arrywe wpone the sodaine, in wiche cais he can not in honor but wise hem well, and keepe to hem the law of nations; and yet, gif he shall gaine the least point of aduantage to the preiudice of ather of our states and common amitie, thenn sall not 10 [Secretary Cecil] and 3 [Lord Henry Howard] be blamles, who sall be mad acquented wyth all hes demands and propositions, and have lasur to schowe hes ansours before thay be put into hes mouthe, and bowt hes flowr before it go to the bakehous. Assur yowr selfe, deer 3 [Lord Henry Howard], if owr intelligence be trewe, thaire ar fewe princes in europe in a worse predicament wyth spaine then our king is at this day.

What yow wreat of sir antonie scheurly may wery well be trewe in a man so ambitius, so much crossed in the way to hes preferment and honor, but what he may prewalle hem selfe or wthers by any acquentance or interest he hath in 30 [King James] is wery well knowen wnto yow, the grownds of hes first profession of seruice to 30 [King James] beinge laid by antonie bacon, as i beleue by yowr priuitie; since that time it is all percian he hes spoken wnto ws, and all papers sent from hem to m. antonie during hes abood in persia were farsed wyth no thing but occurrants in that great kingdome, all utterly improfitable to this poor state.

We lerned that he had a letter wyth a tooken to haue bene presented from hes king to 30 [King James], and I understood at london that he had sent ane sadle to m. bacon for the king; but of all thees we haue receaued no thing but a sownd; as to any messenger from hem, only captane eliot excepted, we had newer non; the duke of mercure hauing recommendid that gentil man to the king, he brought heir a letter from ser anthonie bering the image of hes ouen fortune and what disasters had happened unto hem in hes iowrnay, but of the state of england or spaine we neuer had aduertisment frome hem in hes time: 30 [King James] had never so muche accompte of hem as yow suppose, and, whatsoeuer he hath wndertakine to the spanishe embassadour for hem, he is not bastand [*i. e.* in haste] to acquite hem of suche a charge: yea, i can hard[l]y beleue that

Spain will trwst or imploy hem in such ane action, hawing many fitter agents heir if thair were any possibilitie to effectuat so fine a serwice. I beseche you be not mowed by so lyght and improbable intelligence, for 30 [King James] is setteled upone the center of 10 [Sir Robert Cecil] and 3 [Lord Henry Howard], where yow will find hem rest constant and immowable.*

Yow hawe deluvered wnto ws in the first page of yowr letter a wery scriws and important adwise, wherin we sympathise sowndly wyth yow in opinions, but what prewalls consell whane passion predomings? He is so far a slawe to hes affections that reasonne carieth no more sway, and yow knowe that in so dangerus accidents and inconwenients it is more secure for ws to temporise, nor to repine and disswade. When speats [*i. e.* showers of rain] ar wiolente it is safere to let theme goe then to crose or restange thair cowrs. The more a litle matter is cassine on the fyere, the hottere it bwrins. Our best remedie seems to be to make way to the times and set salles to the tempeste. It may be that tygres turine in turtles, and passion take on compassion, or conterpassion, out of experience, for in hes greatest flammes he forgets not to sasonne soume speches unto [*sic*] wyth acrimonie of hes mynd, ofttims commending the care, the prowidence, the cawtion of 10 [Sir Robert Cecil] and 3 [Lord Henry Howard], howe wiolent a raike thare wits, thare tendirnesse and honestie are set upone, for hes safetie and conseruation; that the smooke of suche colles had not gone so far as wnto them, if sowme fyere wer not smowdered under the ashes at home; that he is ialus of more then ordinarie affection towars hem, that the italien prowerbe may prowe trewe, " who treats me better nor he was wont will, or mynds to, betray me." Suche speches keepe my mind in susspence, so that i am doubfull [*sic*] in what syde of the ballance to lay me in. The wownde, as yow wisly wreat, being so swolled that it needs to be tuiched wyth softe hands, yeat easily curable if corrupt membres wer ather chastised or re-

---

* The intercourse between King James and Sir Anthony Shirley will be found noticed in The Sherley Brothers, 4to. 1840. James addressed a letter to Shah Abbas, King of Persia, on Shirley's behalf: see it, ibid. p. 105.

mouwed. 20 [Earl of Mar] and 8 [Mr. Edward Bruce] stands firme in thair first resolwtion, that to knowe the actours and complices of this farse wer to remedie the siknese and to redeme innocencie frome the graue; if there nams wer discowered, we could mount lyke the iwy and take hold of the branches befor we went to the tope, we could pretend a triall for on crime, and possible wrencte* ane wther out of there finger ends; minte† at on place, and, like good swymmers, hit at ane wther, for we apprehend if on or tuo war commit, that wthers wolde be fugitiue, and so the play breake wp at ons.

Deer 3 [Lord Henry Howard], i neid not bid you be carfull for hes safetie, nor gif your best aduise for prewention of hes parells, since he expects als much loue and‡ tendirnesse from 10 [Sir Robert Cecil] and 3 [Lord Henry Howard] as any living, spetially in maters of this moment tending to hes preseruation.

No address, direction, seal, or indorsement.

No. II.

30 [KING JAMES] TO 3 [LORD HENRY HOWARD].

[HATFIELD MSS. VOL. CXXXV. FOL. 85. ORIG. AUTOGRAPH.]

My deare and trustie 3 [Lord Henry Howard], The cause of my delaye of uryting quhill nou uas only that I stayt upon the parretis cumming, quho repeatid his lesson of *ave cæsar* so coldlie, so careleslie, and aboue all so unperfytlie, that he micht haue bene safelie maid to haue caried his owin death foldit up in such ane œnigme. The deepe and restles caire that both uorthy 10 [Sir Robert Cecil] and ye haue of my safetie I shall neuer be able to recompence, as uell for that honorable and louing dealing of 10 [Sir Robert Cecil] in persuaiding the quene to giue order for the banishement of unquhile gouries brethren, as for his circumspect dealing in the other great

---

* wrench. † aim. ‡ "and" is repeated in the MS.

point, quhairof ye urotte in youre last to 8 [Mr. Edward Bruce]; but as my upricht and guiltlesse conscience hath euer bene my greatest guarde and strong brasen uall, so ame I most sure that thaire is a treacherouse deceate and most uniuste imputation of the innocent usid in that carande, and thairfore, as from the bottome of my hairt I thanke 10 [Sir Robert Cecil] for his uatchfull caire hearin, so doe I praye you most earnistlie to insiste uith him, in my name, that I may be informed from quhat fontaine suche newis are deriued unto him, for by the knouledge thairof I presume I shall be able to guesse at the quhole misterie.

I doe also persaue, by youre letters to 8 [Mr. Edward Bruce], that 10 [Sir Robert Cecil] is uerrie desyrouse to knowe the knichtis name that delt betuixt the duike of lenox and raulie, and thairfore, althoch the knicht him self be a uerrie honest plaine gentleman, for so farre as I can learne, yett knowing that confident truste can no more be seuerid from trew freindshippe then the shaddou can be cutte from the boddie, I uill giue to 10 [Sir Robert Cecil] this further proofe of my confident truste in him by discouerie of this gentlemannis name unto him, quhiche is sir airthoure saunage, not doubting but 10 [Sir Robert Cecil] will conserue this as a freinds secreate, without suffering the gentleman to receaue any hairme hearby, quhiche more uolde interest me in honoure then him in person, especiallie since the gentlemannis nature appeuris to be farre different from raulies, thoch out of zeale to me and affection to his freinde, he coulde not refuse to be trucheman * unto him. Ye shall also informe 10 [Sir Robert Cecil] that I haue neuer harde uorde yett from Hammillton, neither directlie nor indirectlie, since his returne, quhairby I doe guesse that he is not uell pleased uith his ansoure. Mercurie is also cumd doune to the bordoure; hou soone I receaue his lettir I shall ansoure it in euerie point according to the aduyce sett doun by 10 [Sir Robert Cecil]. I hoape makenzee shall be a instrument of some goode seruice to be done against tirone, for I

* interpreter.

fynde him uerrie uilling; but this and all other particulairs I remitte to the fidelitie of 8 [Mr. Edward Bruce] his penne, and doe comitte both 10 [Sir Robert Cecil] and you to the protection of the allmichtie. From falklande the xxix of iuly, 1602.

Youre constantlie assurid freind,
30 [KING JAMES].

Addressed, " 3."

[Fastened in two places with crimson silk, and sealed, also in two places, with the same seal as the previous letter to Sir Robert Cecil, No. IX. p. 27.]

Indorsed by Sir Robert Cecil, " 30 to 3."

No. III.

30 [KING JAMES] TO 3 [LORD HENRY HOWARD].

[HATFIELD MSS. VOL. CXXXV. FOL. 87. ORIG. AUTOGRAPH.]

My deare 3 [Lord Henry Howard], Since my penne is not able to expresse the least pairt of that infinite thankis quhiche my hairte doeth yeelde to my dearest 10 [Sir Robert Cecil] for his so great and daylie desairtis at my hande, I ame forced to employe you as the trustiest freinde to us both to descryue unto him the most uifly that is possible unto you quhat inuarde gratitude both oucht to be, and indeid is, reseruid in my hairte touardis him; but especially quhen I considder the greatnes of his caire and uigilance for my præseruation by his offer for maintenance of a ordinarie guairde, I must saye, uith oure sauioure, that in the last daye he shall stande up and accuse my owin subiects of ingratitude and toe litle caire of me, quho being borne my subiectis by nature, bounde to me by many obligations and benefites, and daylie conuersant uith me, are negli-

gent of that quhiche he, borne a stranger, neuer bounde to me by
any benefite, and uith his eyes neuer hauing seene me, can take no
rest uithout he offer it unto me; but of this, as of all other things,
ye uill by the lettir of 8 [Mr. Edward Bruce] be particulairlie
aquaintid uith my mynde. I can not also thanke 10 [Sir Robert
Cecil] aneuch for aquainting me so uifly with the cogging of graye,
but I have commandit 20 [the Earl of Mar] to make you aquaintid
uith suche a iuggeling trikke of his as maye make both 10 [Sir
Robert Cecil] and you holde in a great quhyle youre expensis upon
phisike by a halfe houris goode lauchter: and thus, my deare 3
[Lord Henry Howard], being for lakke of laisaire compellid to be
shorte, I bidde you hairtely fairuell, euer praying you to reste
more and more assured of the constant affection of
Youre most louing freinde,
30 [KING JAMES].

Not addressed.

[Fastened and sealed in the same manner as the last.]
Indorsed by Sir Robert Cecil, " 30 to 3."

No. IV.

8 [Mr EDWARD BRUCE] TO 3 [LORD HENRY HOWARD].

[HATFIELD MSS. VOL. CXXXV. FOL. 88. ORIG. AUTOGRAPH.]

If i sould afflict yow by my scribbeling, most deer and worthy 3
[Lord Henry Howard], that wndergoes now so great a weight of
bussinese for the good of 30 [King James], i sould heape colles
wpone my owen head, and wery iustly be argued of importunitie,
since the reflex of suche fruits as 10 [Sir Robert Cecil] and 3 [Lord
Henry Howard] trawels produce daylie, ministers almost euerie
moment wnto ws new mater of consolation, all aduertismentꝭ which

we receiwe bering that the counsell and state standeth for ws in a constant and resolut wnion to aduance owr ryghtfull hopes, but frome what springs suche resolution flowes, is als difficule for them to know as the inwndation of nilus; the most i can say to yow is, that happie ar thay that perseuereth to the end.

We obserue yow languise betueen hope and dispare of 24 [Queen Elizabeth's] helthe. Our conceits of both are schortly these. If it sall pleas God to call her presently to hes mercie, we think it sall be dangerus to leive the chaire long emptie, for the head being so far distant from the bodie may yeald caus of distemper to the holl gouernemente; and if so it fall out, 30 [King James] is wery desirus, if your helth can suffer yow, that yow sould come to hem, fraught wyth 10 [Sir Robert Cecil's] aduise in euerie thing that may concerne hes enterie and resort to that croune. Many doubts may aryse wherin non sall be so muche trusted as your selfe. Wyth yow we will frelie confere anent our preparation, our conwoy, our confidence in all men of your state, and of all wther things of most importance to our present fortoune.

Giwe her seiknese relent and continow, so that sche become insensible and stupide, wythout hope to recouer her former helth and capacitie (as is wsuall in suche maladies), wnfite to rewle and to gowerne a kingdome, we would wise according to the cours of common law and exemples of manie kings, that sche being destitut of all reasone and consent, *habens neque welle, neque nolle*, sould be dewolwed *ad agnatos et gentiles*, and that her nerrast kinsman, and most apparent aire, sould be inwest in the tutill and administration of her state; for giwe hir diseise draw long, it is to be feared, that the tuo great kings, your nightbours, out of ambitius emwlation put them in there beast preparation of force and puar to assaille yow by conquise, and mak this holl yle by time the feild of mars; but in this, as in all wther things, 30 [King James] suspends hes owen iudgment and commits hem to the prouidence and care of hes kindest nombres [*sic*], and espetially to hes deerrest 10 [Sir Robert Cecil].

The means ar most politique and wise by which yow hawe dispersed the clowd of ane apparent popise uprore, and it is a wery safe and singular good rewlle, rather to preuent then to be preuented, yet did we trust so muche in your industrie that, giwe thay had gon on to do there worst, yow could hawe pulled suche feathers from there wings as myght hawe mad them come schorte of the great pray they hunted for.

The letter sent from 0 [Earl of Northumberland] to 30 [King James] did arriwe the night befor this packet come to my hands, which was wpon the 23 of this instant. It is wery discretly and temperatly wreattin, and in all points wery nere the trewthe. He says not that he is a catholike him selfe, but that sondrie of hes retenow and dependance hath ores in there bot, and that thay ar not able to resolwe in any cours wyth the whiche he sall not be mad acquented; if it appereth [sic] not wnto me that yow hawe seene her [sic] letter alradie, i sould hawe sent yow the coppie of it in this packet.

As to the proclamation,* it is set of musicke that sondeth so sueitly in the ears of 30 [King James], that he can alter no nots in so agreeable ane harmonie; in reading he weighed all the words of it in the ballane of hes owen head, wyth great affection prasing both the pen and prouident of that counsellour that inspyred suche a resolution. Say to 10 [Sir Robert Cecil] in my name, that, giwe suche a seruice be remunerable, he will find hem selfe ons gratfullie acquat at the hands of 30 [King James].

We intrait yow, all whom yow call heir yowr deirrast frynds, to hawe a care of 10 [Sir Robert Cecil's] saftie in the time of suche riots and tumults as may now arise, when suche changes and alterations ar eminent to the world; as he is carfull to guard ws, so let hem hawe a care to guard hem selfe, that he may be reserued and preserued to ws, *ad meliora tempora*. No doubt but all desperat and wnhappie sperits who longs to see ane anarchie and confusion in

---

* The document which sounded so sweetly in the ears of King James was evidently the draft of the proposed proclamation of his accession to the throne of England, prepared by Sir Robert Cecil and sent to Scotland for the King's approval.

your stat, wil thrist for hes blood and rwine befor all mens in the kingdome, so much the rather that hes inclinations and affections glance heir away. In what sort 30 [King James] sall giwe thankes to the consell for so kind parts as thay hawe giwen proof of and protested towars hem in this time, let hem be aduertised, and whuther by message or by wreat, and when it sall be convenient, wyth all uther circomstances, yow will remember hem.

There is againe ane wther post come from the cyphers of the toure * direct by the sam hand i wreat to yow befor, only to acquent ws wyth 24 [Queen Elizabeth's] estate, and to importoune a spedie sending wpe of 9 [Mr. David Foulis], which 30 [King James] is of purpose to performe if it seeme agreable to 10 [Sir Robert Cecil] and 3 [Lord Henry Howard] wpone the returine of your ansour to hes last dispatche. If there be any misterie in that message, both 9 [Mr. David Foulis] and hutsonne † keepes it from 20 [the Earl of Mar] and 8 [Mr. Edward Bruce], who ar not muche curius of their cours, but if it be lesome ‡ to gesse, becaus hutsonne is now become all our tresoreres man, and sends all his secrets wnto hem, i trust it be some monie mater: i speake this only out of opinion. Hutsonne hes lykways a dealling wyth the wenetien embassadour, who, as he wreats to 30 [King James] and the tresorer, offers in the behalf of the seignorie great aid and succours in monie to 30 [King James] in this time of hes necessitie; whow it shall be performed i am incertaine till i see the euent, but of this I beseiche you returne me nothing, nor let neuer 10 [Sir Robert Cecil] nor 3 [Lord Henry Howard] in any case take notice of it, ather to hutsonne, or 9 [Mr. David Foulis], or any wther livinge.

Efter the date of this dispache you send me now, there was a gentilman direct from richmont the 19 of this instant at 2 hours efter diner, who arriued the night befor your packet lat, and had audience of 30 [King James] in his bed at 7 in the morninge; his credit was

---

* Keepers of the Tower?   † James Hudson.   ‡ lawful.

from Sir Robert Carie to giwe 30 [King James] assurance that 24 [Queen Elizabeth] could not owtliwe thre dayes at most, and that he stayed only at court to bring to hem the first newes of her dethe, and had horses plased in all the way to mak hem speed in hes post. Thus yow see when the great whell of the horologe mowes, all the litle vns runnes a pas; i pray yow let this be imparted to non but 10 [Sir Robert Cecil], for I fear, (say nothing too of the partie) and returne me no ansour wnto this.

30 [King James] keeps heir the greattast modestie and silence that is possible, for thought rumors and speaches comes dayly to hes table of 24 [Queen Elizabeth's] seaknese, he takes no notice of it, nather yet hes he acquented any of his nobilitie, 20 [the Earl of Marr] excepted, wyth hes present condition.

It is thought mete by 20 [the Earl of Mar] and 8 [Mr. Edward Bruce], that yow acquent ws by the next, giwe 30 [King James] sall mak any forces and puar to be in reidinese at all hasards, to oppose and resist against hes ennemies, if any sall happen take armes to inwad and oppose against hes interest.

30 [King James] commends muche your direction giwen to the gward, and wisseth the consell to persist in so good a resolution. He rests in this opinion that, thought he be of mynd to alter no man in any office or charge he possesseth in the stat, yet where it standeth hem wpone the safetie of hes lyfe and suretie of hes personne, the state will yeald hem so muche fauour to grant hem a free election of hes guard, and all members theirof, giwe not skottes at the least inglise, for the common benefit of both the contries.

Thus hawe I deliuered wnto yow my mynd wyth suche schortnese as the necessitie of your bussinese requireth, wissinge yow to mak no schewe of suche perticulars as I hawe imparted wnto yow. I trust yow will keep me in hes wonted fauor to whom I hawe awowed, nixt on, my inuiolable seruice, lyke as to your selfe I sall remaine a constant and inchangable seruant for euer,

           8. [EDWARD BRUCE].

I can not forget that Sr Thomas Challendar hath wreattin a uery kind letter to 30 [King James] in recomendation of your great seruis wnto hem. Lett it serwe yow to know it, and wtherwais I wise yow to take no notice of the same; i would think hem a fite compaignone for your conwoy in case yow did tak couraig to come to this place. Many things i hawe to say whiche I can not wreat; only it will pleas yow yet to excuse 20 [the Earl of Mar,] who parted from ws not tuo hours before the arriuinge of this packet of yours. So long a[s] 30 [King James] sall hawe need of a guard, so long sall it be at 10 [Sir Robert Cecil's] charge; what remains, if so it please hem, sall be reserued and rendered most thankfully whiche I for warrant.

Because of the multitud of advertisments we receiwe, yow most be the more frequent in sending at this time, for we meine to sall by no wther compas then your consell and aduise in all thinges; care neuer whow short yow be to 30 [King James], so yow giwe hem any sence of your meninge, for now he goes not abrood, and longes euerie our for newes from yow; he wold be glad now to read your letter in the worst caracters that euer yow wreat, sence I knew yow [and] your stille.

At my closing, 30 [King James] hes caused 9 [Mr. David Foulis] bring me the coppie of a letter wyth hes ansour whiche it will pleas yow receiue in this packet.

It sall not be amise yow temper 30 [King James's] to great heast in remowing hence in case god call 24 [Queen Elizabeth], out of your selfe or ane aduise of the nombres, for now he burines to be gone.

Againe the lord be wyth yow and prosper all your good and honorable desinge.

7 [Cobham] and ii* ar forlorine in our accompts, and i beseiche yow think not that any subiect in england is able to win grond in ws to the least disgrace of 10 [Sir Robert Cecil], for we ar exceed-

---

* Not identified ; perhaps Raleigh.

ing far inamorat of hem, and yow sall acquent suche as yow lowe of essex fryndes that giwe any of them hawe suche bussinese in heed, or meane to fallow suche a rout, it will turine them assuredly to thir ruine, for this is setteled in the hairt of 30 [King James] ; this only to your selfe.

25 of marche at 6 ours at night.

Addressed, " 3." [Lord Henry Howard.]

[Fastened with green silk in two places, and sealed also in two places with the same seal of Mr. Edward Bruce used to the last letter, and on several previous occasions.]

No. V.

8 [MR. EDWARD BRUCE] TO 3 [LORD HENRY HOWARD].

[HATFIELD MSS. VOL. CXXXV. FOL. 102. ORIG. AUTOGRAPH.]

After the closing of my packet, deer 3 [Lord Henry Howard], 30 [King James] sends on to me wyth diligens to come to hem. At my comming i fynd captaine Selbie wyth hem who parted frome Londoune the 23 of this marche. He deliuered many letters from gentillmen of good accompt, espetially from the tour. Thay certifie all of 24 [Queen Elizabeth's] wery neer approches to her euerlasting rest. The erle of Southhamtoune hes wreatin to 30 [King James] ane arnist letter for a warrant of hes libertie immediatly wpone 24 [Queen Elizabeth's] dethe, wiche 30 [King James] refuseth to grant wythout consent and authoritie of the consell, and is to wreat to hem to deall be way of supplication wyth the consell, and what thay aduise hem to do sall be performed wyth diligence; it is inioined to yow by 30 [King James] to speak wyth 10 [Sir Robert Cecil], and giwe he find it expedient to inlarge hem, and that hes present saruice may be of any wise in the stat, he sall be content, and assents he be presently relewed, wtherways to let hem stay till forder resolution be taken for the best cours in hes bussinesse. We here the erle of Sussex is comming touars ws ; we ar affeard that to manie wesae [*i.e.* visit] ws, and of suche as hath not knowen ws heretofore. Take heed to the maine point, and hawe a care that the citie be mad suore, wther things of lese moment I cease to wreat, being more then werie. I wise yow, deer 3 [Lord Henry Howard], to liwe and die in all happinesse.

"8." [Edward Bruce].

Addressed, "3." [Lord Henry Howard].

[Sealed in two places with impressions on red wax of an oval seal bearing a shield ensigned with the royal crown of Scotland, and containing the following arms,—a lion rampant within a bordure charged with eight fleurs de lys.]

No. VI.

9 [MR. DAVID FOULIS] TO 3 [LORD HENRY HOWARD].

[HATFIELD MSS. VOL. CXXXV. FOL. 103. ORIG. AUTOGRAPH.]

Moast honorable and woorthie 3 [Lord Henry Howard], the tuo last past so suddanly as I could not salut youe, and although I would and could boathe, yit could I say no more then that which I hoape ye are assured of, which is, in a woord, that I shall ever pray for the continewance of your disposition to see the crown putt vpon your owne work, and that I, in spetiall, who owe you so muche for my owne particuler, and others for the generall, as yit unknowne to you, may ever live happy to see bothe you and your busines flouryshe. Fairwell, noble lord, and I pray you love him who lovithe you, and so shal remain with resolution

to serve you,

9. [David Foulis].

Addressed,—"3." [Lord Henry Howard].

[Fastened with a band of paper, and sealed in two places in red wax, with impressions of a seal bearing three leaves.]

PART III.

CORRESPONDENCE WITH THE EARL OF NORTHUMBERLAND.

No. I.

0 [HENRY EARL OF NORTHUMBERLAND] TO 30 [KING JAMES].

[HATFIELD MSS. VOL. CXXXV. FOL. 90. COPY IN THE HANDWRITING OF MR. EDWARD BRUCE.]

SIR,

Since nowe i haue cleered, as i take it, the uay of my letter, I will no longer conceele that affection wyche hetherto hathe been depressed, an affection not resulting from lyght humors, but out of reason, for if i wold say it grew out of your majesties fauours, or wther ocular motiwes that steir seruice to princes, the flatterie would be to grosse, but when I sall say that my conscience tould me of your successiue ryght, and your nixt ryght telles me that you ar lyke to be my king, the originall will be muche mor probable. Nether can I deny that my vndirstanding of your majesties knaulege to iudge betuene good and euell ar the lest additione to it, that can not chuse but promise great hoppes of good from you; the rather when that tottering state of your ouine that hath beene guided thorowghe so many difficulties may serue for ane exemple. So falles it also wythin compas of my reason that the anexing of theas thric kingdomms most ncides be glorius and great for the king that must guueirne tham, striuinge to secure it from hurt or conquist of nighbour princes, and happie for ws, since subiects ar euer soe where largest dominions are.

Nowe that your majestic knouethe the ground of my affection,

I will wndirtake to dissend to the perticularities, not that i am so arrogant as to aduise you, whois syght is muche cleerer in thes secrettes then my weeke iudgment can deliuer, but becaus i may not wreat often, many letters beinge mor subiect to miscarie then one; and, albeid this berithe wyth it nothing that may be improuued dangerus to my person, yet would it be treason to my fortunns if it sould come to lyght; thairfor, if in this ether my opinions sall seeme strange, or tedius, perdon my letter, and censour the wther, I beseiche you, to proceed from the loue of a faythfull seruant to you, and out of a thristinge mynde in me to see this contrie of myne florishe in it selfe, and giue the lau to wther nations about it.

The two mane points that are most in question emongst ws, and that I thinke may giue your maiestie best satisfaction to wndirstand, are theas; the one, whither after her maiesties life your ryght will be yealded you peacebly, wythout blosse [*i.e.* blows], or not? the wther, whether it be lykely your maiestie befor your tyme will attempt to hasten it by force.

For mater of your clame after her maiestie, I here noene almost cawle it in question. Whousoeuer summe bookes of the infantas title be diulged by the factius iesuitts, that mwue litle or nothing, nather can I doubt but your maiestie, from so many as I conceaue are deuoted to your ryght, must needes receaue discouueris of there affections in this nature, and soumme of tham, I doubt not, in this deliuerie of it will make your difficulties appere wyth what art thay can to be many (for suche is the commonne supposall) when soe euer it sall pleas God to caule the queene from amongsst ws; but neither to sifte there endes, whider there arguments be formed frome the treuth of there conceats, or from polliey, to indeere them selues in your fauor, I must conclude that my weeke wndirstanding cannot discerine, as our state now stands, and as it hathe takene wpon it a new face wythin this yeare past, but that you shall als quietly, wythout opposition, haue it yealded, as euer prince had any kingdomme was done to him.

The reasons that induceth me thus to beliefe are theas: the world assumeth a greatar freedom since essex death to speake freely of your title, with the [greater] allouance of it then euer, nor can I marke out any one president that any man is trubled for it, but rather such personns that other facts hathe brought wythin compas of iustice are wyth a gentler hand corrected, if any thing donne for your sake be a part of the offence, wyche to me arguethe that it is not distastfull to the cheefe agents in our state.

At this instante, all mens mynds louking efter there priuate gaine, noe mans ambition is discouered sterring to worke for pouar to be able to oppose agains your ryght, ather by strengthening them selues wyth popularitie, wyth armes, wyth fallowars, or by making them selues masters of the strengthes of our contrie; for plotting wyth any forraine princes, no humwr or circomstance touards it doeth appere, how so euer somme haue beine charged wyth that imputation, an imputation out of myne ouine knowlege rising from the dreggss of former malis [rather] then out of iust cause. When we looke into your competitors at home we finde the eies of the world, nether of the great ons nor small ons, ones cast towards them, for ether in there worthe are thay contemptible, or not lyked for thare sexes, wyshing noe more queens, fearing we shall neuer enyoy an wther lyke to this.

As for the warres of Ireland, the proceedings in them are soe rether held one not to louse what we haue then by any extraordinary expense to gaine what we haue not, this being held for a maxime emongsst vs, that the Irishe will all comme and lay there swords at your feete quhen you sall be our master; and, last of all, what greatter argument can be insisted wpon that we meane not to be your opposite then by leuing the borders soe wneared for, committing the gouernement of them to soe weeke and wnuorthy commanders?

What I knaw of mens affections in perticular were to long now to deleuer, but as all theas things make for me in the conferming me in my opinion, soe, say somme, that there are wther motiues that mak agains me; one is, that the better sort emongsst ws feare your election of consell and instruments onder you to assiste you in the state will be scotts; the other, that the name of scotts is harche in the carres of the wulgar; the last is the faction of papists, that will stand for tolleration of conscience. To the first obiection I haue thus ansured, that for your ouen sake it will be your maiesties labor rather to nourishe vs in quiet than to mouue discontents at your first entrie, that your wisdom will striue more to wnite the tuo nations in all loue, by matches and other politike meanis to make them one, as nowe england and walles are, then to diued them by enuy, wyche wauld be the hazard of bothe there ruins; nether doe I think the kings of scotland haue reason to be so far enamored wyth the fayth of there subiects that willingly thay will repose a greatter truist in them then in the englishe. Besedis, I conceaue it, your maiestie being half englishe your selfe will think that your honor in being reputed a king of england will be greatar then to be a king of scottes.

The second objection is easiliar beaten bake when it is knowen that the wulgar in this case will follow the exemple of there superiors, truisting to there wills rether then to there ouine; and the memoriss of the ancient woundis betuene england and scotland will soune be cancelled when conscience in there harts sall proclame your ryght. For the papists, it is treue there faction is strong, there encrease is dayly, and there diffidence in your maiestie is not desperat. Somme of the purer sort of them, who hathe swaloued the doctrine of putting doune princes for religion, may perhapps be whoter then there ware reason, wishing the enfanta a better se[h]are in the kingdome then your selfe. But since your maiestie vndirstandeth better whow to leede this cause then I can giue instruction, I will dare to say no more, bot it weare pittie to losse so good a kingdome for the not tollerating a messe in a cornere (if wppon that it resteth) so long as they sall not be too busy disturbers of the guuernement of the state, nor seeke to make vs contributers to a peter prist.

Yet is not my scope out of theas circomstances so to ouer assure you that your prouisions be not ansuerable to ane expected opposition, and your resolutions of expedition so concluded, when that sall fall to your turine, that thay [*sic*] may be no giuing of breathe to consult, in wyche your maiestie hath muche the aduantage of any forraine prince, haiuing nather shipps to rigge or contrarie windes or tydes to hinder; and nowe, since it falles wythin compas of my penne, I may not forgett to yeald censure in this point, if not my knowlege, that I thinke her maiestie in the secrett of her heart wishe it you before any creature when she must leaue it.

Nowe to vnfold the arguments we vse emongest vs whetherc it be reasonable and lykely your maiestie will attempt to hasten your ryght by force before your tyme; many of your faythfulest seruants feare, thoghte an exceeding confidence assure me the contrary, whiche I will neuer cease to wishe, for many reasonns.

The motiues that sterres theas feares in your faythfullest seruants are theas; first, your maiestie being a prince of sperite the tyme may be long-seeming wher expectatione of sutche a fortun is at hand; that your maiestie is master of a people great, proper, and apt for any interprysing courses, who will euer vse persuations to be sterring you; that your fryndes and assistants are mani, what out of your allyes by denmarke, the ancient league wythe france, and the irishe, wyche perhapps myght be at your deuotion, ether in respect of thair fault they haue so far plonged them selfes into agains there souueraigne, or out of hope of a more freedome in religion; that her maiestie being in her declinigne age, men louke reather for the soune rysing then efter the soune setting; that the forces of our country is diuerted, somme loukeing after ireland, wthere assisting the loe countrys, and somme few imploying them selfes touars spaine at sea, noen of which may be conueniently neclected, whereby our state wythin our selues is weekened, and that all men are discontented in generall.

The confidence that I imbrace, contrarie and opposite to theas motiues that moues wtheres feares, are thus begott in me with assurance to the contrary; as thay conceaue your majesty a prince of sperit, and princes of sperit are apt to be put on to action, so doe I conceue you withall euer temporat and wyse, not leed by wther mens affections, as hitherto your actions hathe made good testemony of, and a prince not hastaly to ouer throwe so sound a proiect, whos foundations hetherto hathe bene so fermly laid with patience. And, albeit your people are apt and forward to enterprysing courses, desyring spoile of that is not theirs, your maiestie, commander ouer thaire desires, cannot lyke to see the ruine of that is so nere to be your ouene.

For denmarke, what forces or preparation can thaire be sterring that will not sonne be discuuered? How can it be thought that france, for all hes old lague, will be ouer weill pleased to see a prince myghtier then hem selfe at hes elboue? Let the reason be weighed why there league was first confermed, and it sall be founde that it was to lessen england, and not to ade greatnes to it For the irishe, so ruienated and dispeopled in there country, soe poore in there means and soe wvdded to there ouene home by nature, as scarce they could be drawen this last winter out of there bogges and fastnesses to ayde there fryndes that cam into there ouene contry to giue them freedom, what suer hoppes then are to be lenned to of there assistance? Besides, your maiestie is not ignorant that if any of theas courses be discuuered a foote, that your owen subiects, being so prone in there disposition to lay wiolent hands wpone there prince, how easy would it be to find instruments to take yow away, wiche all your seruants could not hinder nor helpe; and if taken away, ether by the fortoune of warre or wtherwayse, in the minoritie of your sonne, he being bot a chielde would hardlie be inwested euer wyth hes ryght in this kingdom, others hawing once taken possession ouer his heade.

If the wery tyme of hir majestie can not be long by the couse [sic] of lyfe, for it is most certaine that yonge boddyss may dye, but old boddys mwst out of necessitie, would the hasard then conterwale the tyme that may be, but perhapps, gained? For the diuiding of our forces into so many bussinesses, soune would thay be recaulled togedder when it sould comme to the question of so essentiall a point: and by the warrs many good commanders ar breede, our selues in generall more fasoned to the humors and myndes of soldiers than euer, all whiche would be empidiments if any attempt should be wndertaken. It is treue, that, of the nobilitie, somme ar not satisfyed, the gentilitie displeased, the men of warre mutters, and the popularitie is grieved, yet lett it be from whence theas discontents doe resulte considered, and thay will be found weeke pillers to adventour soe great ane action vppon.

The nobilitie are wnsatisfied that places of honor are not giuen them, soe sonne as they becomme iudges of there ouene desert; that ofices of trust are not laid in there handes to manage as thay were wont; that her maiestie is percimoniws and sloe to reliefe there wants, whiche from there ouen prodigalities thay haue burdened them selues with all. They repyne that the state walue them not at that rate thay prise themselues worthy of; nether is there many in this ranke, for somme are pleased, and wthers are not capable of them; soe as your maiestic may decerine theas to spring from heat of youth, impaciency, want, and selfe conceate, hote discontents sonne borine and sonne dying in them selues, stings not bitter enoughe to leade them on to soe great a hasard, when there considerations vppon could bloode shall telle them, that that prince wiche sall follow, can not but conclude them in his heart apt to imbrace the sam disloyalties wpon lyke apprehensions: discontents rysing from the ingratitude of humane nature, wyche for the most part forgetts former benefits if wnsatisfied in his last desires. The burden that the gentilitie repines at chiefely is wardschps, a law first instituted for preseruing them in tyme of there minorities, now becomme the ruine almost of all mens houses once in a three dissents; a commoditie smaule in the princes coffers when the accomps ar cast wp; nether doeth this soe farre moue them to discontent, that thay will wentoure the losse of all to redresse this one, both becaus custom hathe made them obedient to it, and hopps giue them beliefe thay may be freed vpon easier conditions hereafter.

The soldier mwtters only when he wants imployment, wiche, in effect, is as muche as when he wants means to robbe the common treasor of the kingdom (by pilling and polling a company of poore creaturs committed wnder his charge) to satisfie the humors of there ryotus excesses; a sort of people that no sonner heres the droume beate but there discontents are quenched, and instantlie becomme lesse servants to a stranger prince, then thay ware when there sworde did hang quietly in the scaberd, soe as i say there conditions are not muche to be relied wpon; of whom to say more, a kind of men fitte to be nurished out of necessitie to help the ministers of a state, rather then to be chosen ministers in a state them selues.

The popular griefes are subsidies, taxes for the warrs, grants of monopolies, and delays of iustice, in all whiche they rether condemne her maiesties instruments wyth the burden of it, then conceaue hatred to her person, this obseruance being almost infallible, that a commonalty may sonner be drawen to rebellions vnder cullor of setting straight iustice, then in aduancing any mans title. I am of opinion that it is mutche easiar for a great man, popular in his ouen coontry, to moue them to commotion, then for your maiestie, if you were so disposed.

Soe as I conclude, all theas circomstances wele laide together, that noen can deny, but that your maiestie shall with out all contradiction enioy that you are soe nighe to by ryght, and that it can not be good for yow, or vs, that you should seeke it sonner by force; for this I haue euer almost noted, that lesser kingdoms seldome kept long a greater gotte by conquist, but by ryght and succession often, for where conquesst runne, the woundes of parents and fryndes blede still fresche in there memories, watching but oportunitie of reuenge, and to free them selues of the burden.

To giue ease to your maiestie from theas weeke discovueryss of myne, I will desiere that what I would say of the borders, of letters seeming to comme from your maiestie, of letters not receaved when they haue comme, of means of sending, that it would pleas you to giue credit to this gentilman, one of my house, an honest man wyth ovt whome I feare me I sould yet haue bene longer sylent touards you; therefor, recommending my honest seruice to your maiestie, he sall kisse noue your handes for this tyme, that will be euer ready to doe you faythfull and trewe seruis when yow pleas to command,

NORTHUMBERLAND.

[The address not copied.]

No. II.

30 [KING JAMES] TO 0 [HENRY EARL OF NORTHUMBERLAND].

[HATFIELD MSS. VOL. CXXXV. FOL. 92 A. COPY IN THE HANDWRITING OF MR. EDWARD BRUCE.]

Ryght truistie cusing, I haue receawed your most wyse plaine and honest letter from the hands of the gentilman berrar herof, and I haue conferred wyth hem at als great lentht as the oportunitie of the tyme could wyth saftie from the hasard of hes discouerie permite: and althoght I neuer douted of the integritie of your affection towars me, for many reasons whiche to the berrar I haue coumwnicated, yet am i infinitlie glaide, that you haue by so honorable a letter, and so weill a chosed messinger, maide the first discouerie therof.

To the tuo maine points of your letter, whiche you conferme wyth many well grounded and infallible ressons; for the first of them, altho it be a maxime in the scoolles that *De futuris contingentibus non est determinanda veritas*, yet by all probable apparance your opinions are well grounded, and I do assuredly hoppe that god, who hathe by lineelle dissente cleede me wyth ane wndoubted ryght to your croune, will also in the deu tyme mak the possessione therof and entrie therinto pleasand and peaceble to me and wnto you all, althoght, as you wysly confesse, I ought notwythstanding heirof omite no lawfull prouision for the most of it * that becommes a wyse and prouident prince to doe in so graue a mater.

And as for your aduyse in the wther point, if my constant resolution ware not agreeable to your aduise,† I could nather be religius, wyse, nor honest, for whow could I be religius to preuent Godes lasare by wnlawfull anticipation, and to doe that wronge to my nyghtboure, the lyke wherof I would be lothe to suffere in my oune person? It ware wery small wisdome, by clymming of diches and hegges for pulling of unrype frvite to haserd the brekeing of my necke, when by a litle patience, and abyding the seasone, I may wyth far more ease and safetie enter at the gette of the garding, and inyoy the fruittes at my plesour, in [the time of ‡] thaire greatest maturitie. Yea, what a folisse part wear that in me, if I myght doe it, to hasard my honor, state, and person, in entering that kingdome by wiolence as an wsurper whiche God by lawfull ryght hath prouyded for me, to the which I am called as a lawfull haire, as § noue in the place of the present quene, wythout inuerting, innouating, or making any alteration in the state, gunernement, or lawes; and besydes, what confidence could I euer heaue in those that for pleasour of me hade betrayede there present soueraine? No, since the old prouerbe is most treue, that, thoght princes mak sumtymes wse of tresone, yet thay euer heate the treatour, wyth what securitie could I think to make my residence in a kingdome so full of treatours? And, last, for the point of honestie, wyth what mask, or waille, could I cover that blot to myne honor, in being the first breker of, for an wntymly ambition, of that long continowed fryndshipe betuixe the quene and me, espetiallie at this tyme, when by my long honest behauiour

---

* In a copy of this letter in the handwriting of Sir Robert Cecil, also preserved in the same volume of the Hatfield MSS. which contains the copy from which we print, we find, instead of " for the most of it," " in case of the worst," which is no doubt right.

† Here Sir Robert Cecil's copy, to which we have above referred, omits the twelve words which occur between " your aduyse " in the preceding line and the repetition of the same words in the above passage.

‡ Supplied from Sir Robert Cecil's copy.

§ Sir Robert Cecil's copy reads " as the sonn of the present qween."

touars her, I haue at last atteaned to a more inuarde and confident amitie wyth her then euc[r] was betuix us heirtofore?

For conclusion then of this letter, as by the chois of this messenger you haue giueine a testimonie both of your honest intension in imploying a gentilman whom nature must binde you to loue, and so not to ingage forder then you may weill warrande him, as also of your wisdome, he beine athere sumthing to you, or nothing to hem selfe, and thairfor doe I heirtlie wise you to employ hereftcr non wther mercurie in your delling wyth me. Yea, forder, wauld I wise you to be ware wyth sending of any message to me at all, except sume great occatione sall require it, least if any misfortonne fele out, it myght breed hearme to ws both; to me in sturring anewe the quenes jalosies, at this tyme so far quenched, and to you in respect of the jaluse state you haue ones stand into. Assur you, ye can by no means so far inhable your self for my seruice agains the laufull tyme as by not only mentcinning, but also aduancing, your credit at her handes, that when ever it sall pleise god to call her to his mercy, you may be a chiefe instrument to assist my setteling in that seate wyche I honor as the apparant heire, in all quietues, wythout the alteration or preiudice of any that will not willfully resist to my ryght. And thus remitting the more perticular discours of all things to the berrers sufficiencie, of whos honestie I haue euer heard a sound report, wyth assurance to your self of my thankfull acceptance of this your so honorable a resolution, and so I bid you heartly fairwell.

    Your louing and affectiona[t] frynd,

            [J. R.]*

---

* The initials of the king's signature are derived from the copy in the handwriting of Sir Robert Cecil, who adds a copy of the indorsement, "The K's lettre to me," shewing that his copy was made from the original, so indorsed by Northumberland. Bruce's copy was sent to Lord Henry Howard. It was addressed "3," and was fastened in two places with crimson silk, and sealed in two places with Bruce's accustomed seal in red wax.

No. III.

0 [HENRY EARL OF NORTHUMBERLAND] TO 30 [KING JAMES].

[HATFIELD MSS. NO. CXXXV. FOL. 95. COPY IN THE HANDWRITING OF MR. EDWARD BRUCE.]

The letter it hath pleased yow to send me doeth so demonstrat the wisdome and justnesse that the world attributs to yow abowe wther princes, and the fauour you hawe done me in accepting a trew construction of that was my faythfull meaning, as i confesse it doethe tye me wyth more deuotion to honor your vertus, wyth nereness to behold them, and wyth integritié to doe yow honest seruice; for in it I find ane approbation of the great law that is the foundation and basis of all laws, all trewe policies, and all commerce, be it emongest cristiens, philosofers or infidells, or wyth kings, magistrats, or inferior persons, I meane that grand law deliwered ws, doe as yee vauld be done wnto, a law that *implicite* in yowr maiesties letter yow limit your self by, and iudge of the actions of wther men.

My last letter, so farre as it concerneth yowr self, inclwdit in it the tuo mane points. I deliwered yow how men might be affected in generall. In this, i hold it not suerwing altogidder frome ordour and conweniencie to gif yow some light how perticular mens affections may be dewoted towars yow; not that I will vndirtake to discouer them as things impossible to be wtherwyse (for so might i diwe into ower great a raschnesse, since time, newe proiects, inconstancies, and deepe dissemblings may giwe a bloe to my censowre,) but as things wery probable to my iwdgment as the circomstances hathe hethereto leede me. Nether will i deliuer all the propositions wiche circomstances and my owen vndirstanding hathe laid togidder towars the conclwsions i am to make, in tuo respects; the on, to eschewe yowr maiestie more trwble, the wther, not to commit to lowse papers sutche a trwst as may wronge my frynds, in being able to say probably against them, thay hawe spokin to freely to Northumberland. But this will i wow to your maiestie, since it hathe pleased yow, as I wnderstand by the partie that last came frome yow, to repose confidence to what i sall deliuer yow, that willingly i will neuer lye to yow in word or iugment, but striwe to giwe yow that case that yow may wnderstand me ewer wythowt difficultie, wythowt labor, wythout iealowsie, becaus the fauor i desir to merit may be permanent, purchassed rather by my plainnese and sinceritie then by indirecte ways, for i knowe deuises must needs perishe when theas will subsist.

I gather by this messinger that yowr maiestie receaws wery often informations of mens affections wery incertainely, wiche must ryse athere out of there ignorance that deliuers them, or out of malice that will detract of them thay lowe not, or owt of partialitie that will giwe to much to them they lowe. Any of theas must be ane impediment to yowr trewe knowlege in the measowr of honor that ewery on bearithe yow, and rarely sall yow find them that will make direct dealing wyth princes the wery grownd plotte wpone wiche they will bwild there credits. I deny not but that they worke the more wnsurly; yet it is sufficient that men for the most parte beliefe not soe, and in this point, since my opinion differs frome the wulgar, i will nether giwe more to my frynds then they deserue, nor conceale that i holde them faltie in concerning yow. The sam measour of indifferencie will i hold towards them that in my owen perticular i doe not affect, since thay and i must be frynds in what dothe tuich yowr ryght, what wther dislykes soe ewer there be emongst ws.

And now that it falles owt in cowrs to speike of perticular men, yowr maiesties iwdgment of essex to be a noble gentilman, but that yow lost noe great frynd by hem, leades me on the rather to this discowrs; to conferme therefor yowr maiesties censour, I must say iustely, that althonght he was a man endeued wyth good gifts, yet was his losse the happiast chance for yowr maiestie and england that cowld befawle ws; for ether doe I feale in my iudgment, or he would hawe bene ane bloody scowrge to owr nation. Of this i can speake wery perticularly, as on whoi [*sic*] was as inward wyth hem as any lywing createur, the first two years i was matched wyth his sister. And could he then dreame of any thinge but hawing the continowall pouar of ane army to dispose of, of being great constable of england, to the end that in an interregnum he might call parlaments to make laws for owr selwes? Did he not decree it, that it was scandalus to owr nation that a stranger sould be owr king? Was not his familiaritie wyth me quite cancellet when he had discowered my disposition leaning to yowr ryght, and that i was not to be leede by hes fortunes? Did he not secretly keepe me frome all preferments of the north parts wyth planting iealusies in the quens mynde of me, whiche are there stille freche when those maters comes in dispute? Did he not euer prefer wthers of more facilitie to hes will then my selfe in any actions whereby i myght come any way to equall hem in the repwtation of a soldier? How often hawe i heard that he enweighed against yow emongest sutche as he conceawed to be birds of hes owen fortoune? Did hes soldiers followars dreme or speake any thing but of hes being king of england? Did his dealings wyth walentine thomas* declare hes affection to your maiestie in theas last actions? Did he not goe to a drynesse with montioy when he would not consent to set wp for themselfes, when he saw yowr maiestie walked wyth causion, and would not be drawin in to be made the brige ower which he would hawe passed for his last refuge? Did he euer offer yow this serwice but in hes declyning time, and at the last pusche? Did he not promise papists freedome in religion, pwritains the swaye of the commonwelthe, soldiers wther mens lands and howses; and those he knewe was yowrs that for yow it was that he wrought for? Well, to conclude, he woore the crowne of england in hes hart these many years, and therefor farre frome setting it wpone your head if it had beine in hes poware. As for cobham and rawlieghe how thay bend towars yowr right this is my censowre, although thay be in faction contrary to somme that howld wyth your title, yet in that point i can not deny but they be of the same myndis, and to rwn the same cowrs. The first of theas tuo i knowe not how his heart is affected; but by the latter, whome six-

* A miscreant who charged James with a design upon the life of Elizabeth.

tein years acquentance hathe confermed to me, I must needs affirme rawlieghs ewer allowance of yowr ryght, and althowghte I knowe hem insolent, extreamly heated, a man that desirs to seeme to be able to swaye all mens fancies, all mens cowrses, and a man that owt of himselfe, when your time sall come, will neuer be able to do yow muche good nor hearme, yet mwst i needs confesse what i know, that there is excellent good parts of natur in hem, a man whoes lowe is disawantageus to me in somme sort, which i cherise rather out of constancie than pollicie, and one whome i wishe your maiestie not to loose, because I wowld not that one haire of a man's head sowld be against yow that might be for yow.

The nixt relation that I mwst enter into sall cŏ[n]cerine the partie that your maiestie required of the messinger whiche was wyth yow how he stood affected towars me, and of whome he assured yow frome me, in what terms i conceawed hem to rest in. The same iugment i gawe of hem then, the sam must i still remaine in. The circumstances that leades me to doe soe (what wther autorities so euer i hawe for myselfe,) i will allege for defence of my opinion, wiche is, that after her maiestie wpon whome he layethe the foundations of his fortenns, that the secrett of his conscience doethe conclude yowr title to be the nixt right, that hes heart will then wishe that it may hawe that approbation with all men, and that for the present he will not be the man to wronge yow, by setting a foote or laboring in any bodise titles whatsoever. The circonstances ar* theas; first, the ancient familiaritie and inwart trust hathe bene betuene ws wiche doethe make hem ondrestand me wery well, his knowlege of my opinion of your title, when necessitie of dethe of our souerainge must lewe it to ane wther hand, his conceawing of my determination to rwnne that cowrse, in setting wp all the faltes of my fortoune that way, yet doeth he continow hes lowe in preferiange me, in frynding me what he is able—besides giwe he hathe aimed at any wthers marke, the matter sould hawe beine caried extreme closhe, that nether i nor non of hes deerest frynds

* " ar are " in MS.

(all wiche i neuer heard ons make almost any question of it) sould not at some time or wthere hawe discoured somwhat. If he sould affect to bring in the infanta, as hathe bene laide to hes charge, wiche waye woold he woorke it, when all hes friends be contraire wyth whome he conwersethe? By hem selfe i know he can not doe' it, and there is nothing more odius in hes nature then suche a thought, upone whiche i will paune my honor, a thing that sowld not slyde wnder my penne but upon assured growndes. This may be forder induced for a comfirmation of that i hold;—was not the clemencie great that hathe bene wsed to all the nobilitie that offendid in this last rebellion, and many wthers that were conceawed to leane towars your majestie? Was it any boddy els that sawed sowthchamtonne? Hes he not mitigated the extremities against montioye, and sowld not essex [haue] gone nere to hawe liwed, if ane assured combustion in our state must not of necessitie hawe fallowed by hes lyfe? If theas then be not sufficient warrants for my iudgment, to conclude that hes heart is not spanishe. i referre it to your maiesties wisdome and submit my selfe to your forder knowlege. Newerethelesse, out of the trust it hathe pleased yow to repose in me, i mwst giwe yow notise, that i can not beleive that euer he will open hem selfe unto your maiestie, wpone any condition, so long as her maiestie liuethe, for he is wery wise, and is not ignorant how harshe a thinge it is to her disposition that any sould think or looke towars a new sonne, nether will he hasard his fortoune wpone so tikkle a ceremonie or pointe, and in my poore opinion in that he merritts iustely an allowance frome yow, for your maiestie knowethe wery will [*sic*] the great place of fauor he now enioyethe; the most he can expect herefter can be nothing neere it, for diuerse reasonns i could allege; men naturally nurishe that thay hawe in hand rather then that thay hawe in hope.

Being fearfull that I hawe ouer wearied your maiestie wyth theis perticularities I will reserve the rest to a longar time, and a larger paper, and if in this clause I hawe beine ernistar then there is cause, to the end it may seme plaine to your maiestie, that yow may not conceawe sinisterly of hes prosedings by other mens reports, bycause I know how necessir a member he may be to your bussinesses, in cherising those that be your honest and faythfull serwants, and i confese that my conceite is that this way he may doe yow more seruis, then if he were otheruyse knowen to yow then he is; he is wery well worthe the esteming, and so doethe he wishe yowr maiestie to doe, that owt of hes lowe and honor to yow, is yowr majesties, to doe yow faythfull and honest seruis.

Nor[thumberland's] Postscript.

Theas three last (spetially the secretary) I hawe begwnne wyth to giwe my censours in tuo respects, the one because i know more perticular circomstances of them then of wthers, the other because i know there may be more iealowsie of them then of any. In my next, i will deliwer my opinion of all the rest of our great men in state; by it, together wyth your maiesties owen secrete knowlege, yow may ayme at ewery perticular mans affection. If that I sall deliuer concwre wyth that yowr maiesties selfe knoweth, it is likely to be trewe; if not, then at lest it will giwe your majestie cause of forder suspence and sherche.

This last attempt wndirtakin by the englishe man wiche now yow hawe in holde, I will assure your maiestie, was receawed emongest ws generally wyth great tendirnesse of yowr person, and wyth many coniectowrs who myght be the instigators, somme fearing it might come frome hence, others from the pope, others frome the frenche kinge, for thay say he hathe a wery great thirsting efter this nation, and lookes wpone it wyth a wery gredie eie, if it sould pleas god to caule her majestie. But to conclud for this pointe, this discowery i hawe wpone it, that i find that willingly we would not that any hearme sould befaule yow.

I fear yowr maiestic hathe somme vntruistic serwants, or vnsecrett, neer yow, for yow stere no where nether doe any thing but we know it. I will therfor to make ane end crawe perdon that this berrer come not to yow at this present. When the nights ar longer he sall attend yowr maiestie to deliwe[r] a great deall of theas maters more at large. I will not faile in the mean time to be a carfull watcheman for yowr maiestie in what may make for yowr serwice hereafter, and intreat yow to hawe a carfull eie to your selfe, for those that lowe yow feare yowre safetie, in whiche more then i hope there is cawse. I wndirstand of late that the citisens ar generally well affected to yowr titell, and soe i conclude thay will goe [wyth] your maiesties right.

Your maiestie may perceaue unlesse my hotte hand be conterfeited heirefter, by this manner of sealling, whiader the letters come wn-oponed to your hand or not, spetially when the letter it self bearethe the subscription whiche in this i could not conweniently doe by reasone of the lengthe of it.

No address or indorsement.

[The copy has been fastened by a band of paper, and sealed, in red wax, with the seal of Mr. Edward Bruce, of which there have been several examples before.]

No. IV.

30 [KING JAMES] TO 0 [HENRY EARL OF NORTHUMBERLAND].

[HATFIELD MSS. NO. CXXXV. FOL. 97. COPY IN THE HANDWRITING OF MR. EDWARD BRUCE.]

Ryght trustie cusing, i am heartly glad that it is my good fortoune to be acquented wyth a noble man cariing so honorable a mynd, as also that doeth ryghtly interpreatte and discerine of my honest in-tensions as yow doe. In both your letters may clerly be seene the wpryght sinseritie of your affection towars me, wiche gif I doe not requyte wyth thankfullnesse i sould more wrong my self then yow. And as to yowr last, wharin yow giwe your censoure of diuers mens affections in particular, I think it not possible to find mor apparent probabilities in a caise of that nature, wharin nothing of certaine can be concluded (*ante ewentum*), but spetially concarninge the cheife agent of that state. I protest I will euer hope for the best of hem, so longe as he trewly serwes the present, and sall worke nothing derogatorie to the futour, and theirfor i cannot bot wery well allow of your inwart fryndchippe wyth hem, as on who can best inhable yow to make your pouar to haue a correspondence wyth your affection in my seruice (*cum venerit dies ille*). If wtherways he disceaue my expectation, I leve it to yowr cawsion to mak hem disceave hem self and non of ws. But although I know that of all men in england, he will be the himmost [hindmost?] to make hem selfe knowen wnto me during the queenes breathe, so great is hes caution, for hes ouen hasard, yeat if he serwe treuly the present and wrong me not in her time, as I hawe alradie said, I can think no wtherways of hem nor of ane wery honest man.

As for his fauorable behauiour to suche personnis in perticular as in your letter you haue wakened out and observed, althought diuerse men may diue[r]sly iuge therof, yet doe I well allow of your cheritable interpretation, and so it fitts best a cristian king to thinke; but your obseruing of their names in perticular puts me in mynd of on of them, poor southamtoune, who liwes in hardest cais of any of them, and if in any sort your means may helpe to procure hem forder libertie or easier ward, pitie wauld prowoke me to recommend it wnto you. I do wery well allow of your warenese to wreat or send wnto me, for a king can not be wythout many eyes wpon hem, as on exalted on a heght and eminent place, and althought I perceaue, both by your letters to me and the erle of mar, that thair intelligences ar false and contryued, yeat amongs many gessings at circvmstances something may runn conter that will foster jalusies, and ane small discoucrie may marre a great game; and therefor as I wreat befor so i man [*i.e.* must] repeat the same, since my cours is honorable and avowable in substance, bewarre to offend the quene wyth schadows, and send no mo messingers except some great and wrgent occation of sending be accompainged wyth some suir and safe means of connoy, in the mean time settling your selfe in that certaintie that, by yowr honorable and faythfull delling, yow hawe acquired the sincere and constant affection of your louing and assured frynd.

No. V.

0 [HENRY EARL OF NORTHUMBERLAND] TO 30 [KING JAMES].

[HATFIELD MSS. VOL. CXXXV. FOL. 99. COPY IN THE HANDWRITING OF MR. DAVID FOULIS.]

Sir, According your commandment I have forborne to present you with my lettres, which now causes of importance moues me to, and I have differred it this long becaus I was willing to see what liklyhood of event it would comme to. Her Maiestie hathe bene euell now almoast one monthe. In the twelve first dayes it was kept secrett vnder a misprision, taking the caus to be the displeasoure she tooke at Arbella, the motions of taking in Tyron, and the deathe of her old acquentance the Lady Notinghame. Those that were nearest her did imagine these to be the reasons. Moer dais told ws it was ane indisposition of bodie; siknes was not in any maner discerned, her sleep and stomak only bereft her, so as for a 20 dayes she slept very little. Since she is growne very weak, yet sometymes gives ws comfort of recoverie, a few houres after threatnes ws with dispaire of her well doing. Phisick she will not take any, and the phisitions conclud that if this continew she must needes fall into a distemper, not a frensie but rather into a dulnesse and a lethargie.

This accident hathe made all the wholle nation looke about them. Men talkes freely of your Maiesties right, and all in generall gevis you a great allowance. The affections of many are discouered to be wholy devoted to your seruice. Euery one almost imbraces yow, for which we that are your trew servantes are glaide of. For myne owne knowledge, I must speake trulye, euery man that hathe offered themselves to me are wholy devoted to your right, and I heere none contradict it, though somme are sylent and say nothing. Thus muche for the generall. For the counsell of the staite, I must lett your Maiesty understand, that they have wrought thus fare touardes an honest and just course with muche lyking of oure whole cuntrye, and I conceave that they meane honestly to your Maiesty. They have called to them some of the nobilitie, at that tyme no more being at court then the Lord Thomas Howard, the Lord Cobhame (who els would haue mutined extremelye) and my selfe, to whome they haue gevin notice of there desyre of oure assistance, bothe in aduyce and other wais, for the good of the state, and depression of suche as wold moue insurrections, if that misfortune of the lose of oure mistres shall happen. Herafter a greater number wilbe summoned, but as yet stopped upon hoape of amendment. In the mean tyme, order is gevin for pressing of all such rogues as might be apt to stirre, and are sent unto the Loe Cuntries; the cityc of Lundonn is commandit to keip strong watch least discontented persones might mak any head theare; the two presidentes in there governementes have the lyke charge, and withall to haue ane eye to the papists. Some recusantes of greattest notte are committed, and commandit, but not with any maner of rigour. Euery countye hathe the lyke wairning. Care is willed to be had by the commanders of the strong places for feare of surpryses; so as they having combined them selves, and meaning to combyne them selves with moe, of whome they cannot be ignorant of the affections of many of ws to your caus, I must needes conclud that they all intend to doe lyke honest and just men.

In all this liklyhood of so mightie a change, not one man hathe sterred sauing Sr Edward Bemanne [Baynham], a wyld and free speaking youthe, who brauing it, and protesting that he wold loose his lyfe, and so wold 40,000 Catholikes more, ere your Maiesty should comme in, this man is committed to prison, and I assure your Maiesty condemned by all of them, ore the most pairt, that are Catholiklye affected, vnles it be by some of them that are puritane papistes that thrist after a spanish tytle. Since we heere no more of them or of that mater (thoughe he hathe laid vniustlie imputation vpon others) as I think, only by naming them ouer whom he nather had power nather vnderstood there hartes.

Somme papists I have in my famylie, who serve me as watches how others are affected, and some that I am acquainted with, but yet did I never heer any of them say but that they all of them wished your Maiesty the fruiton of your right, and that if suplications might procure them tollerations of there contiensces, they should hold them selves happy; if not they must, by the lawes of god and right, endure it with patience; to which hoapes I ever geve comfort that it wold be obteaned; your Maiesty may doe in this case as your wysest judgement shal derect you.

Now, sir, maters standing thus I haue no more to say then that I wishe yow to be ready in as strong a maner as you can (with as litle showe of mouing as you may) to helpe your servants if we find opposition; the dout that I have ordinarly propounded is feare of your entrance in hostile maner, which would geve ane impression of disaster to the people. I must still rest vpon the text of my first lettres, in which I think I shal not muche have erred, and that was, that your maiesty would come in with all peace, with all joy and glaidness to ws all, and free from all opposition.

I have laboured in your vynyard with all the industrie my poore vnderstanding would give me leave. If it shal happen, or pleas god to take from ws oure mistres, you shal have instantly woord, and I think newes of her departure will be no sooner with your Maiesty then woord of your being proclamed amongst ws will ouertake it. I speak it confidently, and therfore I hoope your Maiesty will pardon my ryche [*sic*] thoghts, which are deuoted with eagernes to your Maiestys service and my cuntries good,

NORTHUMBERLAND.

I discover dayly by circumstances that the secretarie is more persuadit to the right of your cause then other. If your maiesty can winne him sure to you, you shall give a great helpe to your busines and to all oure cases. This 17 Marche.

No. VI.

30 [KING JAMES] TO 0 [NORTHUMBERLAND].

[HATFIELD MSS. VOL. CXXXV. FOL. 100. CONTEMPORARY TRANSCRIPT.]

Right trustie and wel belovit cousing, the more I heir from you the more am I reioyced, and do think my selfe infinitly happye that one of your place, endowed with suche sinceritie of loue towardes me, and with all other partes of sufficientie, should be borne one daye to be a subiect vnto me; for I protest vnto you that in your lettre ye have compryced the very somme of all the true newes of the staite of things there, according as I was by dyvers handes aduertised this monthe past. And as to the forme of my entrie there, when ever it shal pleas god to call your soueraine, as in my first lettre I wrot vnto you, so now by these presentes doe I conferme and renew the sam, that is to say, that, as god is my witnes, it never was, is, nor shalbie, my intention to enter that kingdome in any other sort, but as the sonne and righteous aire of England, with all peace and calmnes, and without any kynd of alteration in steat or gouernment, as fare as possible I can. All men that hathe trewlie served there present soueraine shalbe alyk welcome to me as they are presentlye, or wer in tymes past vnto her, claiming nothing in that turne as king of Scotland, but hoaping therby to have the meanes to knitte this wholle Iland in a happie and perpetuall vnitie. As for the catholiques I will nather persecutt any that wilbe quyet, and give but ane wtward obedience to the law, nather will I spare to aduance any of them that will by good service woorthelly deserve it; and if this cours wil not serve to win every particular honest man, my prevy dealing with any of them can availl but lytle. And thus I end, praying [you] for your owne pairt to rest fully assured, that ye shall in the owne tyme have proofe in what hye account ye are with

Your moast loving fryend

JAMES R.

Halyrudhous the
   24 of Marche.

APPENDIX.

PART I.

LETTERS ADDRESSED TO PERSONS UNKNOWN.

No. I.

30 [KING JAMES] TO 40 [AN ENGLISHMAN NOT IDENTIFIED].

[HATFIELD MSS. VOL. CXXXV. FOL. 101. ORIG. AUTOGRAPH.]

Trustie and uell belovit cousin, Althoch youre readines and favourable furtherance to any suiters reccomendit by me, in any thing concerning youre office, euer since youre entrie thair unto, did long ere nou sufficientlie persuaide me of youre honest and lawfull affection to my seruice, yett having laitlie the assurance thairof confirmed, both by the faithfull testimonie of 10 [Sir Robert Cecil], as lykeuayes by youre owin uordes utterid in ænigme to my servaunt ashton, I uolde not omitte to sende you these few lynes of my owin hande, as uitnessis of my thankefulnes, and as by my lettir to you and 10 [Sir Robert Cecil] coniunctlie ye are allreadie certified of my honest and upricht course uith youre soueuraigne, and that I ame no uayes to emploie you beyonde the boundes of youre alledgeance, so have I for the present no other recompence to sende you for youre goode uill but my faithfull promeise that all my dealing uith you shall euer be accumpanied uith these three qualities, honestie, seacreatie and constancie; but as I uill deale with you by no other uaye but by the meanes of 10 [Sir Robert Cecil], so maye ye assure youre self that youre straite and steadfast coniunction with him in my seruice is the only uaye to enable you both thairin, and to disappointe all my maliciouse and undescruid aduersaries; and thus, trustie and well belovit cousin, I bidde you hairtelie fairuell. From falklande the xxix of July, 1602.

Youre louing freind,

Addressed, " 40." 30 [KING JAMES.]

[Fastened in two places with crimson silk, and sealed with two imperfect impressions of the seal of Mr. Edward Bruce, already described at p. 27.]

Indorsed by Sir Robert Cecil, " 30 to 40."

No. II.

MR. EDWARD BRUCE TO A PERSON WHOM HE TERMS HIS COUSIN.

[HATFIELD MSS. VOL. CXXXV. FOL. 104. ORIG. AUTOGRAPH.]

The 24 of September, 1602.

As the laike of meanes, my deer cusine, for the safe convoy of my letters and messages wnto yow was the only cause that to my great greife constrained me to refraine this long time past from wraitting wnto yow, and no cauldnese in my naturall affection touars so nere a kinsman, so doe i now most greatly ioye, hawing found out a way for remedie theirof by the mediation of this honourable gentillman, your cusine Kniftoun. But in a farr greatter measure was my ioy augmented, when i heard by the report of the berrar hereof, my servant, how that nather farr distance of place, nor long abstinence from mutuall intelligence (the only ordinair meanes to breede and nourishe fryneschipe) was not hable to quenche in you thoas sparklis of your naturall affection touars me (whiche beinge in time of your childhood bred in the bon (as the proverbe is) do now bude and break forth in a greattar maturitie when you may with safetie make the sam appeir. Theas few linnes sall only serwe then, to recommend these two points wnto yow, first, that yow will continew in your honest, doutifull and obedient behauiour to the quene your soueraine, and nixt, that yow will persuad your self in a full assurance of my wnfeinyed affection touair yow, wheronto if yow do well, by the law of God and nature I am tyed wnto, as he who both in blood and affection is and sall ever remaine your deerest and neer cousine.

Neither addressed nor sealed.

No. III.

KING JAMES TO ———.

[STATE PAPER OFFICE, SCOTLAND, VOL. 69, NO. 51, 1602? COPY.]

Right trusty freind, Having heard by this bearers report of your honest affection towards me, although I never had the occasion to be acquainted with you, and how you have, for the better inhabling of you to my service, placed your self vppon your great chardge in the nearest adjacent part to my cuntry, I thought it the dewty of a thankfull king to make it knowne, as by theise few lynes of myne own hand I do, my thankfull acceptance of your loving affection, and as I am surely perswaded the only respect to conscyence and vertew hath mooved you to vndertake this course, so may you assure your self that neyther you nor any other of your cuntrymen shall ever be imployed by me without the bounds of the same, as on the other part you shall with God's grace fynd with me a thankfull requytall in the own tyme, as the bearer of theise few lynes, wytnesses of my goodwyll, more at lardge will enfourme you. And thus byds you hartely farewell.

Your loving freind,

J. R.

PART II.

PAPERS RELATING TO ESSEX'S CONSPIRACY.

No. I.

SIR JOHN PEYTON TO THE EARL OF NOTTINGHAM, LORD HUNSDON, AND SIR ROBERT CECIL.

[HATFIELD MSS. VOL. LXXXIII. NO. 86. ORIG. AUTOGRAPH.]

Right honorable, according to her majestyes pleasure singnified in your honors letters, I haue this morning repayred vnto the Erle of Essex chamber, and ther attended vntyll he called for a shirte to shifte hym selfe in his bedde, wher vppon I made knowne vnto hym the cawse of my cuming, and vsed perswading speaches vnto hym toching the delyuery of the Blacke Bagge conceyued to remayne styll abowte hym. And, after I I had harde his protestation to the contrary, in tearmes and manner fitting, I searched his personne, and his boddy, and legges, naked, I allso searched his shirte, and all his apparrell, in such sorte as I doe asure me selfe the pvrse nor wrytyng cowlde not be abwte him, but I showlde haue fownde it. I send vnto your honors herinclosed a resitall of the particuler speaches the Erle vsed in the tyme I was makeing searche for the bagge and papers: most humbly takeing my leaue,

Your honors humbly
JOHN PEYTON.

Towre, this 18 of feabruari, 1600.

Addressed,

  To the Right honorable The Earle of Notingham, The Lord Chambarlayne, and Sir Robert Cecyle, knight, of her Majestyes most honourable priuy Councell.

No. II.

INCLOSURE REFERRED TO IN THE PRECEDING LETTER OF SIR JOHN PEYTON.

[HATFIELD MSS. VOL. LXXXIII. NO. 85.   ORIG. IN HANDWRITING OF SIR JOHN PEYTON.]

That vppon his returne owte of London to his howse, he towke owte of a lettell blacke Taffyta bagge which he alwayes ware abowte hym, a paper the which he protested contayned not in quantytye abowe a quarter of a sheet, and that in it ther was not abowe vj or vij lynes.

That it was an aduertysement sent vnto him, and not of his owne hande, but wryten by an other man.

That ther was not anything in the pursse but onely that paper and a kye of a lyttell Iron cheste, in which ther was a booke of his trobles, all wryten with his owne hande.

That he had an other lyttell Iron cheste wherof the kye was loste, the which he brake open, and towke owte of it diuers priuate papers and letters, that no mans Ii euer saw but his owne.

That he at his returne to Essex howse had in his pockett a cathaloge of diuers names all wryten with his owne hand.

All these abowe specified he protesteth he threwe into the fire and burnte, in the presence of my lady his wyfe, the lady Riche, and the lords and knights and gentelmen that were with him, and as he thinketh Sir E[d]ward Baynham sawe hym burne them.

No. III.

HENRY CUFF TO SIR ROBERT CECIL.

[HATFIELD MS. VOL. LXXXIII. NO. 99 (2).   ORIG. AUTOGRAPH.*]

Righte honorable, my most humble dewtie premised, it is nowe highe tyme that hee whome publicke iustice hathe pronounced the childe of deathe shoulde with the soonest laye asyde all cares of this life, reserving

---

* This letter has been printed in Hardwicke's State Papers, i. 372, but with many inaccuracies, and one most serious omission. I do not scruple therefore to reprint it from the original.

CAMD. SOC.   M

him selfe wholly for that one which the only autour of life hathe honored with this testimonie, that *vnum est necessarium*. For the better attending whereof, and avoyding all future worldly distractions, I have resolved, vpon your honours commaundment, to perfourme this last dewtie by writing, which of late I have often wisshed to have tendred to your honour by worde of mouthe. At the tyme of my last examinationn in this howse it pleased your honour to demaunde of mee the summe of those Instructions which my late Lord and Master had made ready against the comming of the Scottish Ambassadour, whome hee dayly expected. Being at that tyme wholly possessed with exceeding greefe, I coulde yeelde your honour and the rest of the Lords verie small satesfaction. In regarde whereof I have ever since muche desyred somme private accesse to your honour, but being vtterly out of hope of so greate a favour, and being nowe called on by Mr Lieutenant to performe my promise made vnto your honour at the tyme of my condemnationn, I have thoughte it necessary to presente vnto your honour the effecte of those instructions, obseruing, as farre as my memorie will serve mee, the verie wordes and methode of the originall it selfe.

Instructions for the Earl of Marre.

That the king his master thoughte it necessary to beseeche her majestie to declare his righte to the successionn of this Crowne, not because hee observed in her majestie any wante of princely favour and affection towardes him, but because hee hathe founde by infallible proofe that somme very gratious with her majestie, being of extraordinary bothe power and malice, will not fayle one daye, if God prevente it not, to make theyre advantages of the vncertaintie of successionn, not only to the preiudice, but also to the evident hazarde, and almost inevitable ruine, of the whole Ilande.

For proofe of theyre power there needeth no longe discourse, all meanes in all partes and quarters of this realme being in a manner wholly in theyre handes. In the West, Sir Walter Raleighe commaunding the vttermost province, where hee maye assure the Spanyarde his first landing, if that course be helde fittest, being also captaine of the Isle of Jersey, there to harbour them vpon any occasionn. In the East, the Cinq Portes, the keyes of the realme, are in the handes of the Lord Cobham, as likewise the Countie of Kente, the nexte and directest waye to the Imperiall citie of this realme. The treasure, the sinewes of actionn, and the navye, the walles of this realme, being commaunded by the Lord Treasurer and Lord Admirall, bothe these greate officers of state and the rest above named being principally loved by the principall Secretary, Sir Roberte Cecill, who for the further strengthening of him selfe hathe established his owne brother, the Lord Burghley, in the government of the Northe partes; and in the Presidentship of Wales nowe voyde will vndoubtedly place somme body who shall meerely acknowledge it of him. As likewise, in Irelande, hee hathe already procured for Sir George Carewe that province, which of all others is fittest for the Spanyardes designes, in whose handes, if the commaunder himselfe maye be beleeved, there is a greater army then hee needeth; to omitte that the sayde Sir George is shortly in expectation to succeede to the governement of that whole kingdome, vponn the recalling of the nowe Lord Deputye.

That theyre malice towardes that King was no lesse then theyre power, it appeared, first, that somme of them had given directe proofe of theyre ill affectionn by ill offices, &c. [This pointe was lefte to the Ambassadour because the Earl of Essex was enformed that the King was able to produce cleare evidence thereof.]

Secondly, because all theyre counsayles and endevours tende to the advancement of the Infanta of Spayne to the successionn of this crowne.

This pointe was confirmed by nine arguments:

1. Theyre continuall and excessive commending of the excellencies of the Infanta, and seeking by all meanes to breede bothe in her majestie and in all others an extraordinary good opinion of her.

2. The earnest seeking to revive the Treatie lately brokenn, notwithstanding it was interrupted by the Spaniarde not without somme disadvantage offred to this crowne.

3. The speeche of a principall Councellour* to ann honorable personage, That thoughe hee knewe there coulde no sounde peace be made betwixte vs and Spayne, yet, for the better compassing of somme purposes hee coulde be willing to entertayne the Treatie againe.

4. The slacke and easy hande that hathe benn lately caried towardes the priestes of the Jesuiticall factionn, of all others the most pernicious, which

* As I remember he sayde he meante it of your honour.

cann have no other interpretationn but that the popishe faction favoring the Infanta, which are in effecte as many as the Jesuites cann prevayle with, mighte depende onn them as on theyre cheefe protectours.

5. The speeche of Mr Secretary to a Councellour of state that hee coulde prove the Infantaes title to be better then the Title of any other competitour to the Crowne.

6. The speeche of the Lord Treasurer, who, vponn newes that the Archeduke was hurte, and, as somme thoughte slayne, in the laste yeares battayle at Neuporte, answered that if hee were slayne hee thoughte her Majestie had loste one of her best frendes.

7. The alterationn of theyre proceeding with Alabaster, and one Rollstone, who have alwayes founde more and more favour since they professed them selves to have ben agentes for Spayne.

Two more reasons there were which I cannot nowe call to minde. Whether amongst so many other thinges of importance wherewith hee lately acquainted your honour and the rest of theyre Lordships any of these reasons and Instructions were by him remembred, I know not; only, because your honour and theyre Lordships did at that tyme earnestly presse mee to delyuer the summe of them, I have endevored to give your honour the best satisfaction I coulde, being verely perswaded that this abstracte dothe in sense very little differ from the first draughte.

Of myne owne particular, being no lesse destitute of hope then of comforte in this worlde, I dare saye nothing. Only I beseeche your honour let it not be thoughte presumptionn to adde thus muche in generall; That, if the Kinge of Kinges thoughte it for his glory, whenn hee founde least merite to extende his greatest grace, your honour will accounte it no small resemblance of that divine paterne, if his royall lieutenantes, and theyre principall ministers vponn earthe, having layde prostrate humble offendours at the feete of Justice, shalbe contented to surrender vp the sworde of Justice into the handes of Mercie. Thus most humblie beseeching your honour to vouchesafe mee your favourable opinion at my last farewell out of this miserable worlde, I rest

Your honours most humble and
most distressed suppliant,
Henry Cuffe.

No. IV.

HENRY CUFF TO SIR ROBERT CECIL.

[HATFIELD MSS. VOL. LXXXIII. NO. 99 (1). ORIG. AUTOGRAPH.]

Sir, In answere to your demaunde I saye, in briefe, the thinges were not sente, but reserved to be presented to the partie vpon notice of his approache to this towne, to which purpose my Lord was thincking of somme well-qualified confident to addresse vnto him, by whome, as hee shoulde have vnderstoode the full resolutionn of the principall partie from whome hee was sent, so hee meant to governe him selfe in concurring in more or lesse correspondency with hym. Somwhat I coulde happily ghesse at, but I am lothe to be bolde in coniectures vnlesse I did more truste myne owne judgment. I beseeche you most humbly to remember my only suite of this worlde. For wante of paper I ende. Your dayly and dutifull beadesman, H. C.

No. V.

HENRY CUFF TO THE COUNCIL.

[HATFIELD MSS. VOL. LXXXIII. NO. 88. ORIGINAL AUTOGRAPH.]

A true answere to suche articles as were proposed vnto mee on Satturday the [*blank*] of February, by the Lords of her Majesties most honorable privie Counsell.

Moste honorable, my moste humble dewtie remembred,

1. Whereas it hathe pleased my late dearest Lorde and Master the Earle of Essex, for the discharge of his conscience, to delyuer his vttermost knowledge touching sondry pointes greatly importing her Majesties service, referring him selfe likewise to my knowledge touching the sayde pointes, and charging mee, as in the sighte of God, fully to reporte what I have knowenn in the same, I doe here tender vnto your Lordships this true and sincere narrationn, observing the same order which it hathe pleased your good Lordships to retayne in proposing the foresayde articles.

Firste, concerning the Lord Montioyes intelligence with the King of Scottes, neyther cann I saye muche, neyther can I avouche any sure grounde wherevponn to founde that little which I have hearde, only thus muche I remember I have benn tolde, that one Henry Lea was thoughte to have benn his negociatour there, but whether by lettre or only message, or to what especiall purpose, I cannot affirme.

2. Concerning the intelligence of my Lord of Essex with that King, I cannot certainly affirme howe longe it hathe continued, but sure I am that it hathe benn for at least these two yeares. The intent thereof, on his Lordships parte, as I have alwayes conceyved, hathe benn principally that by assuring that Prince of his good affectionn, suche as mighte stande with his soueraine duty to her majestie, whereof hee made especiall reservation, he mighte staye him from irrelegeous courses in declining from his religion, which of late hathe benn somwhat feared; nexte, that he mighte the better hinder the designes of the Infanta of Spayne, whose pretensions to the successionn of this crowne in many respectes hee did vtterly mislike. From his Lordship I have seene one only lettre directed to that kinge, conteyning well nighe a whole sheete of paper, the principall partes whereof (as I remember) were these; first, an apologie for him selfe touching suche vniuste accusations as have benn layde vpon him by his opposites, whose iniurious dealing he complayneth of, and not the leaste that they have soughte to possesse his Majestie with misconceipte of him, as if hee purposed to aspire to that whereunto hee coulde by no colour nor likelyhode iustly pretende. Nexte, a request to that king to employe here somme well qualified and confident person, well instructed, with whome his Lordship mighte securely conferre. Lastely, hee concludeth with a very devout protestation of his duty and zeale towardes her sacred majestie, vowing that hee woulde rather endure many deathes then consent or suffer that any one iote of her iust souerainty and autoritie shoulde in her tyme be impayred; thereby (as I conceave) the more precisely limiting his love towardes that prince, least hee shoulde peradventure expecte more then was intended.

3. Concerning the intelligence betwitxe these Lordes, Lord Montjoy and the Earl of Essex, especeally touching the pointe of favoring the Earles accesse to her majestie, I cann saye little in particular, but must referre my selfe either to Sir Charles Davers, who purposely tooke a

iourney into Irelande to negotiate herein with the Lord Deputy, or to my Lord the Earle, who I doubt not receaved ann ample relation from him of the whole. Only this I knowe, that Sir Charles founde him very affectionate to the Earle, as thincking the publicke to suffer with his private, and consequently that his retourne to her majesties former grace woulde tourne to the good of thousandes. The particulars I omitte, because I maye be mistaken in relating them.

4. My meeting with Sir Charles Davers at Oxforde was by his Lordships apointment, to signifie vnto him, that whereas hee meant to passe over into Irelande there to conferre ioyntly with the Lord Deputy and the Earl of Southampton for the benefitte of my Lord of Essex, certayne newes was comme that my Lord of Southampton was arrived in the Lowe Contreyes; wherevpon hee was againe to advise howe hee woulde dispose of him selfe. In conclusionn hee resolved that him selfe woulde continue his iourney into Irelande and woulde cause Mr. John Littletonn to passe into the Lowe Contreyes to the Earl of Southampton, if my Lord of Essex so thoughte fitte, thence to recall him as soone as conveniently hee mighte.

5. Howe longe the designe for my Lords retourne to the Court hathe benn in hande I cannot precisely saye; only I remember that soone after his Lordships keeper was remooved, Sir Charles Davers had accesse vnto him. What passed betwixte them I knowe not; for Sir Charles tolde mee that hee was expressely boundenn by the partie from whome hee was to deale with my Lord not to acquainte any mann with the contentes but his Lordship only. Howbeit, soone after I observed that matters grewe to have some forme, the Earles purpose therein I doubte not but your Lordships have fully vnderstoode from him selfe. So farre as I had any lighte of it, it was precisely this, to assure his comming to her majesties presence, there to caste him selfe at her royall feete, and with a most humble and dutifull forme of speeche to beseeche her majestie the renewing of her most gratious favour; to remonstrate, likewise, the cruell courses helde against him by his opposites, as subornation of wittnesses to bloudy endes, practising to counterfeyte his hande, and suche like vndue courses, whereby they endeavoured, eyther to dispatch him, or at leaste to make him vtterly odious to her majestie, which hee esteemed a very hell in this life; force, so God be my saviour, there was never intended to my knowledge, nor any other countenancing of the cause by the confluence of the gentlemen

his folowers, but only this, that nothing mighte be attempted against him before his accesse to her majestie. The kylling or so much as the hurting of any one councellour, or mann of qualitie, I have hearde him moste earnestly disclayme, and I ever beleeved it. Hee hathe, likewise, protested vnto mee, before God, that it was neither ambition, nor desyre of private revenge that moved him to desyre this his repayre to the court, but that hee resolved, as a votary, to employe the reste of his dayes in her majesties services, with extraordinary zeale and diligence, abandoning whatsoever had before ben an impediment to him in that behalfe. One principall cause of his differring it so longe after his firste cogitations I take to be this, partely that hee had at sondry tymes receaved somme lighteninges of hope, that her Majestie intended gratiously to call him againe to the courte, and partly because there have benn diverse expectations of a parlament, which in all likelyhoode woulde, if any thinge, have given him oportunitie of accesse.

6. The summe of that which I delyuered to Sir Henry Bromely is this; that I had seene in a lettre from France, for so I thincke I termed it to him, mention made of a Scottishe ciphre, wherein were charactares for the principall councellours of this state, and besydes for two private gentlemenn, namely, Mr. Anthony Bacon and him selfe; I assured him that this lettre was in Mr. Secretaries handes, and therefore willed him not to be to busy in matters of that nature.

7. From the same knighte I likewise receaved, that one Gourden, a Scottishe priest, was able to avowe that x thowsande crownes, if I be not deceaved in the summe, were consigned in France from the Archeduke to Mr. Secretaries vse.

8. What passed betwixte Sir Henry Nevill and my Lord of Essex at theyre firste meeting I proteste I knowe not, only I ghesse there passed little more then complementes and foreyne occurrences, but hereof your Lordships maye be fully advertised by my Lord him selfe.

9. At Sir Henry Nevills conference with my Lord of Southampton my selfe was not present; only I doe perswade my selfe that the plotte for my Lorde of Essex his repayre to the courte was there imparted to him, and his advise required.

10. Touching pretended greevances I cann adde nothing to that which at that tyme I signified to your Lordships, neyther in deede hathe it sorted

with my course of life to fall often into company of suche persons as mighte enforme mee of particulars of this kynde. In myne owne private fortune I professe with all thanckefull acknowledgment that I never receaved the leaste iniurie, neyther at the handes of any of her majesties most honorable privie councell, nor any other personn of qualitie about the courte, but contrary wise many honorable favours, from the daye of my leaving the vniuersitie, till the daye of my committing; which, howsoeuer it hathe benn bitter to fleshe and bloude, yet, by the merites and mercie of my blessed Lorde and Saviour, I finde that to the inner man it hathe benn the beginning of a farre greater ioye and comforte then all the pleasures and prefermentes of this life coulde procure.

Your most honorable Lordships
most humbly at commaundment,
HENRY CUFFE.

No. VI.

THE EXAMINATION OF HENRY CUFFE THIS 2 OF MARCHE 1600.

[DOM. STATE PAPER OFFICE, 2 MARCH 1600-1, ORIG.]

He confesseth that the matter concerninge the Earle of Essex writing to Scotland was debated about Christmas last by the Earle of Essex, the Earle of Southampton, Sir Charles Danvers and this examinate, and that the minute of the lettre was agreed on between them, and that John Littleton was acquainted with this councell. And that this examinate was imployed to meet Sir Charles Danvers this last sommer at Oxforde, to whom he caried a lettre from the Earle, where they twoo conferred at the Crosse Inne and agreed that Sir Charles Danvers should goe into Ireland and deale with the Lord Mountioye, that if the Lord Mountioye could not come over himselfe, that he should wright a lettre to the Earle of Essex which he might shewe to the Quene, concurring in fynding fault with the present gouernement, but with this condicon that it should not be shewed to the Quene vntill the Earle of Essex were come to her presence, for which purpose he should sende over diuers captaines and menne of qualitie, such as he could spare, presuming that, those captaines and menne of qualitie being at the Court before hand, my Lord and his company cominge to the Court might not be resisted neyther by the Captain of the guard, or the guard, or any other. And sayth that the Erle expected that when he cam to the Court he should come in such peace as a dogge should not wagg his tongue against him. And sayth that, after Sir Walter Raleighe had bene removed, the Earle of Essex made a proiect that Sir William Russell should be Capteine of the guard, and after Sir Robert Cecill should be remoued, Sir Henry Nevill or Mr. Bodley should be secretarie, but Mr. Bodley was not holden so fitt. And further it was agreed between Sir Charles Danuers and this examinate that Sir Charles should send John Littleton to London to the Earle of Essex, to be sent over into the Lowe Countries for the Earle of Southampton, who then was newlie come out of Ireland. And further saith that he first heard it of Sir Gellie Mericke long before this, that the Lord Mountioy had sent to the King of Scottes, by Henry Lea, which he tould uppon this accident in excusinge my Lord Mountioy, not to have dealt coldly with the Earle of Essex, for that he had then some other thing to doe for him. He confesseth that Norton the bookseller caried the Erle of Essex lettre to the Scottish Kinge, which Norton received at the handes of the Lord Willoughby at Barwike, and that one part of the lettre was to persuade the coming uppe of the Earle of Marre to London by the first of Februarie. And that the Earle of Essex had under his own hand wrightten instructions to the Erle of Marre, which the Erle of Essex burnt. And this examinate was acquainted that the King of Scottes shuld retourne his annswere in disguised woordes of thre bookes,* which the King did accordinglie. And that was it which the Earle caried about him in a blacke purse. He hath often heard that Anthony Bacon † was an agent between the Erle and the King of Scottes, and so he was accounted.

HENRY CUFFE.

Examined before us—
    THO. EGERTON, C. S.   T. BUCHURST.
    NOTINGHAM.   RO. CECYLL.

* Here at first followed, " viz. Garrie Lonyes,"—but these words were afterwards struck through.

† Here followed originally " conveyed diuers lettres from the Erle to the King of Scottes," but these words were struck through and those which follow substituted in their place.

No. VII.

WILL OF HENRY CUFFE.

[HATFIELD MSS. VOL. LXXXIV. NO. 1. ORIG. AUTOGRAPH.*]

Dispone domui tuæ.

There remayneth in Sir Thomas Conisbyes handes, due at the third day of May next, for the one half of the fyne agreed on for the farme of Bodnam D'eureux, three hundred and fifty poundes, which I desyre may be layed out for the best vse of my noble Lord and late maisters daughters, the Lady Francys and the Lady Dorothey D'eureux, or of ether of them, as it shall seeme best to my deare Lady and mistress the Countesse of Essex. Concerning the money [1700^{li}] which my honorable and trew freind Mr William Killigrew standes bound to pay to Sir Henry Nevill and Mr Henry Savell,† I desyre that it may remayne in Mr Killigrewes handes vntill Michaelmas next, he payinge fowre score poundes only for the vse thereof. Afterwardes, when he and the aboue named Sir Henry Nevill and Mr Henry Savell shall thincke fitt, I desyre that theise payments may be made.

First, to Sr Henry Nevill knight, or to any of his children, as Mr Killigrew shall thinke fitt, the somme of five hundred poundes which I pray him kyndly to accept from his poore distressed freind, whose exceedinge greife it is, that he hath by his late maisters commaundment been an occasion of his trouble, which I pray him most hartily to forgive me.

With the like affection I desyre that there may be given to my trew and deare freind Mr Henry Savell one hundred poundes, and I beseech him to contynue the memorye of his vnfortunate freind, and ever to thinke charitably of him, howsoever some endevour to ruyne and deface as well his name as his estate. I desyre, likewise, that foure hundred poundes may be lefte in the sayd Mr Henry Savells handes, for the space of three yeares, and that he will, after that terme is expired, employ it to the best

---

* I presume that this document had no legal validity, having been written after the testator's conviction of high treason; but it is full of indirect information respecting Essex's party and friends, and alludes to many well-known persons. On the whole, I think it will be deemed well worthy of publication.

† Of course, this was the future Sir Henry, the editor of Chrysostom, and Provost of Eton.

vse of my two Nephewes, Jhon Cuffe and Adame Cuffe, of whose education I beseech him to haue such a care, and likewise Sir Henry Nevill, as they shall thinke fitt.

I doe likewise pray that one hundred poundes may be given to my poore aged mother, as the last remembrance of my bounden duty.

I doe allsoe desyre that one hundred poundes may be given to my worthy freind Sir Jhon Peyton, Lieutenant of the Tower, at whose handes I have founde all kynde favours and Chrestian comfortes, ever since my remoue to this place.

I doe allsoe desyre that two hundred and fiftye poundes be given to Merton Colledge, to buy yearely ten poundes revenue, or more, to be bestowed every Wednesday, as Mr Leech hath ordayned for every Tuesdaye, and the commemoration or *derige* to be allwayes on Lammas day, betwixt such fellowes as shall be present at eveninge prayer that day. The land lett it be bought in any place, but my desyre is that in remembrance of my deare freind (with whom I doe assuredly trust to meet shortly in heaven), Mr Thomas Savell, it be bought in the dyocesse of Yorke.

I desyre that to Mistresse Dorothee Sproxton there be given twenty poundes.

The like somme to Mistresse Thomasyn Carew.

Lastly, I desyre that fortye poundes be given to my honest freind Jhon Norton the bookeseller, as well to discharge the debt I owe him, as allsoe to give him some recompence for the trouble which this great tempest (I feare) is like to bringe vppon him.

As for the remaynder, videlicet one hundred and fiftye poundes, I desyre it may be given to my trew freind Sir George Carye, her majesties Thresorer in Ireland, which I desyre him to accept for a full discharge of all debtes betwixt him and me.

And for the fowrescore poundes due from Mr Killigrew, I beseech him to bestow one halfe of it betwixt ten such personages, men and woemen, as he knew to loue and affect me, his wife and two daughters beeinge comprised. The other halfe I desyre him to bestow *in pios vsus*, by the advise of Mr Savell.

It remayneth that I only add—O Lord, into thy handes I commend my spiritt, for thou hast redeemed me, O God of Truth.

HENRY CUFFE.

APPENDIX. 93

No. VIII.

HENRY EARL OF SOUTHAMPTON TO THE COUNCIL.

[HATFIELD MSS. VOL. LXXXIV. NO. 16. ORIG. AUTOGRAPH.]

My Lordes,

I beseech your Lordships bee pleased to receaue the petition of a poore condemned man, who doth, with a lowly and penitent hart, confess his fautes and acknoledge his offences to her Maiesti. Remember, I pray your Lordships, that the longest lyuer amongest men hath but a short time of continewance, and that there is none so iust vppon earth but hath a greater account to make to our creator for his sinnes then any offender can haue in this world. Beleeue that God is better pleased with those that are the instrumentes of mercy, then with such as are the persuaders of seuere iustice, and forgett not that hee hath promised mercy to the mercifull.

What my fawte hath been your Lordships know to the vttermost, wherein, howsoeuer I haue offendid in the letter of the law, your Lordships I thinke cannot but find, by the proceedinge att my triall, that my harte was free from any premeditate treason against my souerayne, though my reason was corrupted by affection to my frend (whom I thought honest) and I by that caried headlonge to my ruine, with out power to preuent it, who otherwise could neuer haue been induced for any cawse of mine owne to haue hazarded her Maiesties displeasure but in a trifle: yet can I not dispayre of her fauor, nether will it enter into my thought that shee who hath been euer so renowned for her wertues, and especially for clemency, will not extend it to mee, that doe with so humble and greeued a spirite prostrate my self att her royall feete and craue her pardon. O lett her neuer sufer to bee spiled the bloud of him that desiers to liue but to doe her seruice, nor loose the glory shee shall gaine in the world by pardoninge one whose harte is with out spott, though his cursed destiny hath made his actes to bee condemned, and whose life, if it please her to graunte it, shallbe eternally redy to bee sacrifised to accomplish her least comandement.

My lords, there are diuers amongest you to whom I owe particular obligation for your fauors past, and to all I haue euer performed that respect which was fitt, which makes mee bould in this manner to importune you, and lett not my faultes now make mee seem more vnworthy then I haue been, but rather lett the misery of my distressed estate moue you to bee a mean to her Maiesti, to turne away her heauy indignation from mee. O lett not her anger continew towardes an humble and sorowfull man, for that alone hath more power to dead my spirites then any iron hath to kill my flesh. My sowle is heauy and trobled for my offences, and I shall soon grow to detest my self if her Maiesti refuse to haue compassion of mee. The law hath hetherto had his proceedinge, wherby her iustice and my shame is sufficiently published; now is the time that mercy is to bee shewed. O pray her then, I beseech your lordships, in my behalf to stay her hand, and stopp the rigorus course of the law, and remember, as I know shee will neuer forgett, that it is more honor to a prince to pardon one penitent offender, then with seuerity to punish mayny.

To conclude, I doe humbly entreate your Lordships to sound mercy in her eares, that therby her harte, which I know is apt to receaue any impression of good, may be moued to pity mee, that I may liue to loose my life (as I haue been euer willing and forward to venture it) in her seruice, as your lordships herein shall effect a worke of charity, which is pleasinge to God; preserue an honest-harted man (howsoeuer now his fautes haue made him seem otherwise) to his contry; winn honor to yourselues, by fauoringe the distressed; and saue the bloud of one who will liue and dy her Maiesties faythfull and loyall subiect.

Thus, recommendinge my self and my sute to your Lordships' honorable considerations, beseechinge God to moue you to deale effectually for mee, and to inspire her Maiesties royall harte with the spirite of mercy and compassion towardes mee, I end, remayninge,

Your Lordships most humbly,* of late SOUTHAMPTON, but now of all men most vnhappy,

H. WRIOTHESLEY.

---

* The Earl at first here signed his name "H. SOUTHAMPTON," but afterwards erased it and substituted the following.

No. IX.

HENRY EARL OF SOUTHAMPTON TO SIR ROBERT CECIL.

[HATFIELD MSS. VOL. LXXXIV. NO. 18. ORIG. AUTOGRAPH.]

Sir, because I receaued a charge from you and the rest of the Lords, when I last spake with you, that I should conceale the matter which was then in hand, I thought fitt to acquaynt you with what I fownd this morninge by the Liuetenant,* who, talkinge with mee, made mee see that hee knew as much as I could tell him. From whence hee had it I know not, but I protest before God I haue trewly obayed your commandement, and haue not opened my mouth of it to any, nor say this to bringe blame vppon any, but only to free my self from imputation.

But now, seeinge my cheef hope is in your desier to effect my good, next vnto the fauor of God and the mercy of her Majestie, I cannot but remember you of thease particulers, which before I had forgotten. First, that the owld matter, as soon as I could acquaynt my Lord of Essex with it I did, lettinge him know that it was only thought of in respect of him, and how that with out his approbation it should bee desisted, in which hee was so farr from diswadinge that hee gaue mee the directions I haue made knowen. Then, the thought of that beeinge abandoned, hee sent directly for mee into the Low Contries, lettinge mee know, before my opinion was asked, that hee had resolued it. Lastly, to make you see that I was neuer willing to stirr in thease thinges, thise same morninge the matter happned between my Lord Grey and mee,† I telling him that I thought, in respect the thinge was so notorius, the counsell would take notice of it, and send for mee aboute it, hee answered mee that it was lyke enough, but if they did with out question it was but a collor to lay handes of mee, and therfore wished mee not to goe; to which I replied, that he should not enter into any violent course for mee, for I knew I had made no fawle, and I would trust in the iustice of the state; so, beeinge sent for, I only tooke two with mee and went. Now, out of thease circumstances, I beseech you make your coniecture, whether I was likely to bee an instigator in these businesses. For this that I haue sett down, I protest before God is trew, and I

---

* Sir John Peyton.   † An encounter in the public street.

doe rely so much vppon your fauor that I doute not but you will make vse of them for my aduantage, and I shall continew bound vnto you, as I protest I doe account my self alredy, more then to any man lyuinge, which whether I liue or dy I make the world know to your honor. I beseech you pardon the bad writinge of this, for I write in hast.

No. X.

CONFESSION OF HENRY EARL OF SOUTHAMPTON.

[HATFIELD MSS. NO. LXXXIV. NO. 19. ORIG. AUTOGRAPH.]

Att my first comminge out of Ireland and vppon the committment of my Lord of Essex, my Lord Mountioy came to my lodginge to Essex howse, where hee tould mee that hee had before his cominge foreseen his ruine, and desieringe to saue him if it mought bee, had sent a messenger to the King of Skottes to wishe him to bethinke him self, and not suffer, if hee could hinder it, the gouerment of this state to bee wholy in the handes of his ennimies; and if hee would resolue of any thinge that was fitt, hee should find him forward to doe him right, as farr as hee mought with a safe conscience and his duty reserued to her Majestie; that hee expected, within a while after, to receaue answer, which when hee did I should know it. Not longe after hee towld mee hee had heard from him, and shewed mee a lettre which hee sent him, wherin was nothinge but complimentes, allowinge of his reseruations, and referringe him for the matter to the bearer, who deliuered vnto him that the King would think of it, and putt himself in a rediness to take any good occation; whereuppon hee sent him againe with this proiect, that hee should prepare an army att a conuenient time, declare his intent, that hee would bee redy to assist him with the army in Ireland, whether hee was goinge, and mought for the healfe of those doe that which was fitt in establishinge such a course as should bee best for our contry, houldinge euer his former reseruations. Att this time I lykewise wrote a lettre to the Kyng professinge my self to be willinge to doe him seruice, as farr as I mought with my alleageance to her Majestie, and by the messenger sent him woord that in this course I would assist him with my endeauors and my person.

To this dispach wee receaued no answer duringe the time of his aboade heare; but within a while after, the messenger returned, and brought for answer that hee lyked the course well, and would prepare him self for it; but the yeare growinge on, and it beeinge thought by Sir Charles Danvers that the army of Ireland would suffice alone, I made my Lord of Essex acquainted by lettres, hee becinge then att Essex howse, what had been doon, and that opinion hee allowed of, and it was resolued that I should breake the matter to my Lord Mountioy att my cominge into Ireland, which I did, and hee vtterly reiected it as a thinge which hee could no way thinke honest, and diswaded mee from thinkinge of any more such courses, which resolution I toke and wrote ouer to Sir Charles Danvers heere what I fownd, and that I had geeuen ouer thinkinge of such matters; wheruppon, willinge to spend my time in her Majesties seruice, to redeem the fault I had made in thinkinge that which mought bee offensiue to her, I was desierus to seat my self in Ireland, so that the Deputy makinge a motion to mee to stand for the gouerment of Conagh, I desiered that hee would moue it, meaninge, if I could obtayne it, to settle there; which beeinge denied mee, and I vnable to lyue att so great a charge as I could not chuse but bee att there, I resolued presently to goe into [the] Low Contries, leauinge him, and parttinge my self without any imagination (as I protest before God) to thinke any more of any matters of that nature, but resoluinge to take my fortune as it should fall out, and as by my meritt hir Majestic should hould me worthy; or, if the woorst happined, that her Majestic should continew her displeasure against mee, which I hoped would not [be], to retire my self into the contry, and liue quietly and pray for her. I doe protest also before God, I left the Deputy, as I thought and so I assure my self, resolued to doe her Majestie the best seruice hee could, and repentinge that hee had euer thought that which mought ofend her.

I went into the Low Contries with that mind, and so continewed vntill, a few dayes before my comminge thence, Mr. Littleton came to mee, as hee sayed from my Lord of Essex, and towld mee that hee was resolued on the course which is confessed for his coming to the Courte; att the hearinge of which I protest before the Majestic of God I was much trobled in my harte, yet because hee protested in it all sincerely and loyally to her Majestic, I sent him woord that I would att any time venture both my fortune and life for him, with any thinge that was honest. Vppon my first seeinge him hee confirmed as much, and what passed afterward concerninge that I nead not speak of, it beeinge so well knowen.

Mr. Littleton lykewise towld mee that Sir Charles Danvers was sent into Ireland by my Lord of Essex to perswade my Lord Mountioy to write a lettre to him, wherin hee should complaine of the ill goucrment of the state, and to wishe that some course mought be taken to remooue from about her Majesties person those which weare bad instrumentes, protestinge that it should neuer bee knowen till hee had been with her Majestie and satisfied her of his intent, and then hee would shew it her, that shee mought see that not only him self, who perhappes shee would thinke desiered it by reason of his discontentmentes and priuate offences, but also those that weare in good estat and in her fauor, wished to. I then towld him that I did not thinke my Lord Deputy would doe it, for I lett him know how I left him, and that I did not thinke there was any spiritt in him to such a course. Within a while after I came into England, Sir Charles Danvers returned, and towld me that hee fownd my Lord Deputy much against any such course, and that hee had sett his hart only vppon followinge of the Queen's seruice, and thought not of any such matters; but if hee would neades runn that course (which hee did not lyke and gaue him [for] lost in) hee should send him woord, and hee would write to him; this hee towld mee hee yealded to very vnwillingly, and withall towld him, that if any there of his followers would goe ouer, hee would not hinder them.

For that which was proiected for my Lord of Essex eskape out of my Lord Kepers house, I protest before God I alwayes diswaded from it; and the same eueninge before, not three howers before it should have been attempted, I protested against it vnder my hand, and so brake it, incurringe much imputation amongest them for want of affection to my Lord, and slackness to doe him good.

This haue I sett down all trewly as I can remember it, without ether wronging any or fauoringe my self; and will only conclud with this, that I protest before the Almighty God I neuer sett any of these thinges on foote, or beeinge proiected did instigate any to folew them, nor neuer bare disloyall or vnreuerent hart to her Majestie, but was drawen into them meerly by my affection to my Lord of Essex, whom I thought honest to her and to her state; and, had I not been invited when I was in the Low Contries to this last woorke, for which I was directly sent by my Lord of Essex, the world should haue wittnessed with me the duty I had borne to her Majestie, and I did not then doute but with my honest endeuors in her seruice in few yeares to haue deserued forgiueness of my former offensiue thoughtes, which I am now by my accursed fortune cutt of from. I doe therfore now prostrate my self att her Majesties princely feete, with a trew penitent sowle for my fautes past, with horror in my conscience for my offences, and detestation of mine owne life if it bee displeasinge vnto her. I doe with all humility craue her pardon. The shedinge of my bloud can no way auayle her; my life, if it please her to graunt, shall euer bee redy to be lost in her seruice, and, lett my sowle haue no place in Heauen, if euer I harbour thought in my harte which I shall thinke may bee any way offensiue vnto her, but remayné to the end of my dayes as honest and faythfull a subiect vnto her as is in the world; and I doe on the knees of my hart beseech her Majestie not to imagen that these are the worrdes of a condemned man, who, fearinge death, would promise any thinge, and afterward, beeinge free, would as soon forgett it. O, no! The world will wittness with mee, that in her seruice I haue geeuen sufficient testemony, more then once, that I feare nether death nor danger, but they are protestations that proceed from the honest harte of a penitent offender. O, the Kinge of Heauen hath promised forgiueness of their sinnes that with sorrow and fayth aské pardon, and I that doe know her Majestie to be gratius, and doe with so greiued a mind begg forgiueness, cannott dispayre, but hope that the God of Mercy, who doth neuer shutt his eares to the afflicted that cry vnto him, howsoeuer they haue offended, nor is euer weary of beeinge compassionate to those which vnfaynedly repent and call to him for grace, and hath promised forgiueness of sinnes to those that forgeeue in this world, will moue her Majestie to pyty mee, that I may lyue to make the world know her great meritt and serue her; for whom I will euer pray and lyue and dy her humble loyall and faythfull vassall.

[*Unsigned.*]

There bee two thinges which I haue forgotten to sett in their right places, your Lordship must bee therfore pleased to take them in this postscript. One is, that not longe before the day of our misfortune my Lord of Essex towld mee, that Sir Henry Neuill, that was to goe embassador into Fraunce, was a man wholy att his deuotion, and desiered to runn the same fortune with him, and therfore hee towld mee that hee would appoint him to come to my lodginge in Drury Howse, and I should make him acquainted with his porpose of goinge to the Courte, which I did ackordingly, after this manner: I towld him that I vnderstood by Cuff (who had lykewise made mee know his disposition) that hee had denoted him self to my Lord of Essex, and that hee desiered to engadge him self in any thinge wherby his fortune mought bee re-established. If it weare so, I had somewhat to say to him from my Lord of Essex, and therfore wished him to lett mee know his mind. Hee answered mee, that what Mr. Cuff had sayed hee would performe, therfore desiered mee to say on. So I deliuered vnto him what my Lord of Essex intended, which hee allowed of, and concluded that when hee shonld bee appointed, hee would bee att the Courte before, to gyue him fartherance with himself and his people. The other is; that not longe agoe my Lord of Essex wrote to the King of Skottes which hee shewed mee, of three sides of paper and more, the effect of which as I remember was, to discredite the faction (as hee termed it) contrary vnto him, and to entreate him to send hether the Earle of Marr with commandement to folow those directions which hee should geeue, and with all in what woordes hee should geeue him notice if hee would performe it; which hee receaued, and that was it hee ware in the blak purse aboute his necke. Hee drew also, as hee towld mee, instructions for him against his cominge, but I neuer saw them. Thus haue you, I protest before God, all that I remember, or doe know, wherin I once again beseech your Lordship to marke, that I haue neuer been mouer nor instigator of any of these thinges, but drawen into them by my best frendes.

No. XI.

DECLARATION OF SIR CHARLES DANVERS.

[HATFIELD MSS. VOL. LXXXIII. NO. 108. ORIG. AUTOGRAPH.]*

About a month after my Lord of Essex' fyrst commitment to my Lord

* Birch published a portion of this most valuable document (Mem. Eliz. II. 470) from a copy of a copy which is in the Advocates' Library. It is obvious to the most superficial reader that Birch's publication is strangely incomplete; after a certain time it is a mere confused jumble. I am not aware that the paper has ever been printed entire. In vol. lxxxiii. of the Hatfield MSS. there is the original draft as well as a fair copy, both in the handwriting of Sir Charles Danvers. I have printed from the latter.

Keepers, I came from my howse in the contry to London. Before my comming I fownde that, by my Lord of Southampton and my Lord Montioye, vnto whom it seemed my Lord of Essex had comitted, the care of his fortunes, (according to the feares had been conceaued at seuerall tymes of his daiuger to be carried to the Tower,) diuers courses had been thought of for his deliuery, ether by procuring him means to escape priuately into France, or by th'assistance of his frends into Wales, or by possessing the Courte with his frends to bringe him selfe agayne to her Majesties presence. These things had, as I take it, been rather thought on, then euer well disgested, till within ten dayes after my coming vp, vppon a new feare of his imprisonment in the Tower, my Lord of Southampton, my Lord Montioye and my brother, meeting at my Lord Montioye's howse where I was present, it was resolued by them, and approued by me, that it was his best course, if he fownde him selfe in such dainger, to make a priuate escape.

It was proposed by my Lord of Southampton to my Lord of Essex, whether by letter or message I knowe not, with offer that he and my brother woulde accompany him in his flighte. The awnswere my Lord of Essex returned was, as I remember, that if they coulde thinke of no better a course for him then a poore flighte, he woulde rather runne any dainger then leade the lyfe of a fugitiue. While these things were in treaty, my Lord of Southampton, after he had made me knowe how far he woulde aduenture him selfe for my Lord of Essex, that he woulde aduenture his lyfe to saue him, and enter into banishment with him if need were, demaunded of me, how far I woulde engage my selfe for his sake. My awnswere was, that I loued him best, and did confess my selfe to be most behowlding to him of any man liuing. He had saued my lyfe, and that after a very noble fashion. He had suffred for me, and made me by as many means bownde vnto him, as on man coulde be bownde vnto an other. The lyfe he had saued, and my estate and means whatsoeuer, he shoulde euer dispose of. I ought a duty to the parson of my souveraine which I assured my selfe he woulde lykewise respect; I ought a respect to Mr Secretary to whom I had been very much behowlding, and therfore woulde not be engaged in any thinge agaynst his parson. I knwe his Lordship was to noble, howsoeuer he might enterprise vnlawfull things, to attempt any thinge fowle or ignominious. Within these limitts did I engage my selfe to any aduenture of lyfe or estate whatsoeuer. And thus much I knowe my Lord of Southampton in his honor will affirme. Vppon this grownde I was made preuy to all which afterwarde was thought on or proiected.

I offred my Lord of Southampton, when he fyrste thoughte of going away with my Lord of Essex, to waight on him if he woulde, or if he lefte me behynde him, I woulde sell all that I had, to my sherte, to supply him with means to mayntayne him selfe the better abroade.

When my Lord of Essex woulde haue gone away out of my Lord Keepers howse, being aduised thervnto, as I haue harde, by Sir Christopher Blunte, my Lord of Southampton determining to goe with him if he woulde needs goe, though he approuved not the course, I made the lyke offer. Vppon this grownde of affection and thankefulnes to him, ether tendring his safety or endeuoring to free him out of the dainger wherin he was wrapt, I protest hath proceeded whatsoeuer I haue ether intended or acted. To returne where I lefte.

While these things were in handling, the certayne tyme I doe not remember, my Lord Montioye imparted to my Lord of Southampton and my selfe, that the sommer before he had written to the King of Scotts by H. Lee, the particularetyes of which letter or instructions geuen to him I doe not remember that my Lord did euer deliuer particularly to me, but by that which fell out afterwarde, I conceaue it was to assure the King that my Lord of Essex was free from those ambitious conceipts which some of his ennemyes had sought to posess the worlde with all; to geue assurance that next after her Majesty he woulde endure no succession but his; and to intimate some course for his declaration during her Majesties tyme. The cause that mouved my Lord Montioye to enter into this course with Scotlande, and to proceede therin afterwarde, was, as he protested, his duty to her Majesty and his contry: for he coulde not thinke his contrye safe, vnless by the declaration of the successor it were strengthned agaynst th'assaults of our most potent ennemyes, who pretended a title thervnto: nor he coulde not thinke her Majesty so safe by any meane as by making her owne kingdome safe by that vnion agaynst theyre attempts now.

When the gouverment of Irelande was imposed vppon my Lord Montioye, his former motiues growing stronger in him, by the aprehension of my Lord of Essex' dainger, whose case he seemed exterordinaryly to tender, being pressed lykewise ernestly by my lord of Essex to thinke of some course that might releeue him, my Lord Montioye fyrst swearing him selfe and exacting the lyke othes from my Lord of Southampton and my selfe, to defende with the vttermost of ower lyues her Majesties parson and gouverment, during her lyfe, agaynst all parsons whatsoeuer, it was resolued to sende H. Lee agayne into Scotlande, with offer that if the King woulde enter into the cause at that tyme, my Lord Montioye woulde leaue the kingdome of Irelande defensibly guarded, and with 4 or 5000 men asiste that enterprise which, with the party that my Lord of Essex woulde be able to make, were thought sufficient to bringe that to pass which was intended. Whether it woulde haue fallen out that the Kinge shoulde haue entred hostilly and parsonally into the Realme, or shoulde only haue cowntenaused the action with his Embassador, I doe not knowe, for I was only made preuy in substance what was meant; but sure I am that my Lord Montioyes desire was that he shoulde shew him selfe only vppon the borders, and by his embassador's assistance make all men see that the enterprise was for th'establishment of the succession, and not for priuate ambition. H. Lee came not back till my Lord Montioye was in Irelande, and when he came was comitted. What awnswer he brought I am not able particularly to sett downe, but by that which I haue vnderstood I doe iudge, that the Kinge was ether not ready, or coulde not resolue to declare him selfe till the garrison was settled at Loughfoyle, which were the men and shipping intended for that enterprise.

While H. Lee was in prison, my Lord of Southampton went into Irelande, and by him were letters sent from my Lord of Essex to my Lord Montioye, to moue him to bring ouer those former intended forces into Wales, and from thence to proceede on to th'accomplishment of the former designe. My Lord of Southampton for his parte, as I conceaue, was willing to secure him selfe of the feare he had by discouery of the former negotiation by H. Lee, then in prison, to bee vndoon. But my Lord Montioyes awnswere was (which I vnderstood in substance before, but more particularly from him selfe in Irelande,) that he thought it more lawfull to enter into such a cause with on that had interrest in the succession then otherwise, and though he had been lead before, out of the oppinion he had to doe his contry good by the establishment of the succession, and to deliuer my Lord of Essex out of the danger he was in, yet now his lyfe apeered to be safe, to restore his fortune only, and saue him selfe from the dainger which hunge over him by discouvery of the former proiect, and to satisfye my Lord of Essex' priuate ambission, he woulde not enter into an enterprise of that nature.

My Lord of Southampton when he went into Irelande tooke my promisse (within those limitts before specefied) to doe as much for my Lord of Essex as his cause shoulde require, and my power coulde perfourme, vppon which grownde I wrote to my Lord of Essex about the ende of Aprill or beginning of May, not long after he had receaued my Lord Montioyes awnswere. The effect of my letter was to signify the promiss I had made to my Lord of Southampton, that if he had any cause to vse me I might knowe it, for within a shorte tyme I was pourposed to goe into the contrye. His awnswere was that at that tyme he had no cause. Not long after I sent him woorde, that my Lord of Southampton had a desire to pass out of Irelande into the Lowe Contryes, and from thence to sue for leaue to trauell farther. His awnswere was that he desired not he shoulde goe far, for though they were then reiected they might be of vse on to an other. These too, as I remember, were all the letters which passed betweene my Lord and me before my going into the contry, which, in respect of the marriadge of my Lord Harbert and other occasions which fell out, was deferred much longer then I intended. In the meane tyme of my stay, Mr Cuffe, repayring to me as he was vsually accustomed, had diuers tymes speech with me discoursiuely of my Lords fortunes, what issue they were lyke to haue, what he had cause to beleeue therof, and that if he were reiected he thought he might fynd interrest in Scotlande, where it seemed my Lord helde intelligence, whether by some seconde meane or directly I am not able to say.

In this mean tyme I vnderstood both by him and others that my Lord, then expecting euery day to be deliuered from his keeper, was desirus to speake with me before my going away. Not long after my Lord was deliuered from his keeper, Mr Cuffe brought me woorde that my Lord was desirous to speake with me. I awnswered that I was lykewise very willing to satisfy my Lord of his frends carriadge towards him during the tyme of his restrainte. The tyme was apoynted; and I, by Mr Cuffe, was brought vnto him. The substance of my fyrst speech was to lett him knowe how his frends hade been vnto him during his restrainte, for that they had harde that he had condemned them of slacknes and cowldues. What the causes were that he was not satisfyed for his going out of Yorke howse, nor by my Lord Montioye in his last requeste, I assured him from them that they had been and euer woulde be very faythfull frends vnto him. I towlde him more ouer that I pourposed vnless vnexpected busines hyndred me, to goe into Irelande to see my Lord of Southampton and my Lord Montioye, vnto whom I had promised as much; that I knwe they woulde be glad to heare that he conceaued rightly of theyre meritts towards him, and iff he woulde sende vnto them any thinge ells of the state of his fortunes I woulde deliuer it vnto them. After my Lord had awnswered these things, particularly in awnswering the imputation had been layd vppon him of condemning them, and protesting that he esteemed them the best frends he had, and woulde euer runne a comon and vnited course with them touching his owne fortunes, as I remember, he sayd, that at Michelmas the lease of his wynes ended, which was the greatest parte of his state, that by the renuing it, or taking it from him, he shoulde judge what was meant him; that about that tyme he expected there woulde be a parlamente; that if then he were not restored to his place and offices, wherof he seemed much to doubt, he wowlde for his owne parte geue ouer the hope therof. I remember very well he towlde me, that for his owne particular he coulde content him selfe with any fortune, but desired me to strengthen my determination of going into Irelande, and that I shoulde communicate with his frends such things as he woulde thinke of for the good of his contry, and for theyre common good and safety. Before my going from him I remember he fell agayne wppon the drawing ouer of the armye. I wished him to putt that out of his mynde; what reasons soeuer there were besyds, I knwe my Lord Montioye woulde neuer assent vnto it. He then fell vppon this proiect of the courte, and vppon some courses by parlament, which, as I remember, he did not explane. I awnswered him I woulde deliuer any of those proiects to his frends consideration. He towlde me that he woulde thinke more of them, and woulde lett me vnderstande his mynde more particularly, by Mr. Cuffe, before I went, or by letters after I were gone. This, as neer as I can remember, was the substance of the conference betweene my Lord and me.

Within a day or two after, Mr Cuffe came vnto me to my mothers howse at Kensington, ether the day or the day before I went away into the contrye, and towlde me that my Lord desired I woulde howlde my resolution of going into Irelande, to communicate what he had thought on heer with his frends there. If they approuved it, it was desired that my Lord of Southampton shoulde come ouer, and that my Lord Montioye, for my Lord of Essex better iustification in whatsoeuer he did, shoulde wryte a letter of complainte of the misgouverment of the state, and a sommons to my Lord to doe somwhat to redress it. My awnswere was, that I did not thinke my Lord Montioye woulde write so fully in that subiect as was required; that within few dayes I woulde sende to Mr Secretary to lett him vnderstande of my pourpose to goe into Irelande; that if it were approuved by him, as I did not thinke but it woulde be (which he shoulde perceaue by his awnswere which my footman shoulde deliuer him) my Lord hauing thought throughly in the mean tyme what he woulde haue to be deliuered to his frends, might geue me directions accordingly. I harde that my Lord of Southampton was gone out of Irelande, whervppon I sent vp agayne that the greatest parte of the occasion of my going was taken away, both for myne owne desire and for the busines my Lord required, that therefore if it pleased my Lord I woulde stay, and that at the returne of my Lord of Southampton they might resolue together what was fittest to be doon for both theyre goods. Mr Cuffe was returned to me to Oxforde with my Lords request that notwithstanding my Lord of Southampton's departure I woulde proceede in my iourney, and commucate the proiects with my Lord Montioye, and procure his letter. I was still of opinion that my Lord shoulde fyrst expect the returne of my Lord of Southampton, I woulde, notwithstanding, to satisfy my Lord goe on if by the returne of my footman, whom I then sent to London, I shoulde fynde my Lords resolution continwe.

My footman brought me the continwance of my Lords desire, whervppon I went on. I communicated my Lords requests and proiects with my Lord Montioye, whose answere was, that he did not aprouve the proiects. He desired my lord to haue patience, to recouver agayne by ordinary means the Queen's ordinary fauor, that though he had it not in such measure as he had had heertofore, he shoulde content him selfe. That at his coming home he woulde doe for him lyke a frende, that he hoped my

Lord woulde doe nothing but that which shoulde be iustefiable in honor and honestie. In that confidence, if he sent for a letter, he woulde sende him such a one as he might iustefye. After my coming back I imparted to my Lord of Essex my Lord Montioyes requests according as I had promised my Lord Montioye I woulde doe, in very effectuall sorte. I imparted lykewise that it was my brothers oppinion, and I sayd as much to my Lord of Southampton. And for some tyme I did not fynde that my Lord did resolue of this or any other proiect, but hoped at the parliament to be restored in some measure to his fortunes. And not long before Christmas, when it was feared by some of his frends that he shoulde be comitted, in respect of the resorte vnto his sermons, there was more thought of flying then enterprising in this sorte. But from a littell before Christmas or thereabouts the resolution was taken, as in my former confession is declared.

Your Lordships most humbly to comaunde

C. DANVERS.

[*Indorsed*]

1 Martij 1600. Sir Charles Danvers' declaration.

No. XII.

[EXAMINATION OF SIR CHRISTOPHER BLOUNT.]

[HATFIELD MSS. VOL. LXXXIII. NO. 82. ORIG. SIGNED BY SIR CHRISTOPHER.]

The Examinacone of Sir Christopher Blunt, knight, taken before those whose names are vnderwritten.*

He confesseth that at the Castle of Dublin in that lodging which was once the Earle of Sowthamptons, the Erle of Essex purposing his returne into England, advised with the Erle of Sowthampton and him self, of his best maner of going into England for his securitie, seing to goe he was resolved. This was some fewe daies before the Erles iorney into the North.

At that tyme the Erle propounded his going with a competent nombre of soldiers, to the nombre of 2 or 3000, to haue made good his first land-

* The names were not added.

ing with that force vntill he could haue drawen to him self a sufficient strength to haue proceeded further. From this purpose this examinat did vse all forcible perswasions, alledging not onely his own ruine which should follow thereof, and all those which shold adhere to him in that action, but vrged it to him as a matter most foule, because he was not onely held a patrone of his country (which by this meanes he shold haue destroyed) but also shold haue layed vppon him self an irrecoverable blott, having bene so depely bound to hir Majestie, to which disswasion the Erle of Sowthampton lykewyse inclyned.

This dessein being thus disswaded by them, then they fell to a second consideracone, and therein this examinat confesseth that he rather advised him, if nedes he wold goe, to take over with him some competent nombre of choyce men, who might onely haue secured him from any committement to prison, if he had not found hir Majestie gracious, except it were no further then to the howse of the Lord of Canterbury, the Lord Keeper, or his vncle.

After this Examinat came to London, and heard amongst some of his honorable frendes that my Lord had an intention to free him self and come down into the country, he said he was sory that he had not held on his course, fearing by that he had heard him speake many tymes before of the King of Scotts, and of the protestacone of the Kinges love to him, that he might some waye haue endaungered him self by practise there (so farr) as to be in daunger of his lyfe, which he knew then his own conscience must have accused him, that his former disswasion and advise of his maner of coming, had bene the occasion of his coming into that daunger whom he loved so derely. Wherevppon this Examinat with others had once resolved with others to haue freed him, and caryed him awaie, with some 60 horse into Wales.

He sayeth on Saterdaie there was no certein daye sett down for his rysing, more then that it shold haue bene done betwene that and the end of the terme.

But afterward, when Mr. Secretary Harbert had bene there, then there fell questions what was fitt to be done for his securitie, and so it was resolved by some (if there were a newe sending) that he shold goe into the citie, of which the Erle made him self most secure by such messages as he told this examinat had bene sent vnto him that night, but from whom particulerly he is loth to venter it on his conscience, but by the sequell it apeared to be the Sherif Smyth, whom before the Erle had often named vnto him, that he was a Collonell of 1000 men and at his commaund.

For the matter of Lea, he confesseth, that he had order from my Lord to let Capten Thomas Lee goe to Tyron whensoever he shold come to him to require it, and afterward Lee came to him at London, and told him my Lord wold haue this examinat take it vppon him which was after my Lord had bene charged with it before the Lords.

That in all proiectes of blood, whensoever there was any plottes spoken of, he protesteth on his sowle he was ever a disswader,* [when vpon advyse he had thought of it, though when sutch courses wear spoken of he gaue hys allowance ageynst the Secrettary, whear, vpon my solle, I presenttly repentted me, and never after gaue my allowance to any villany of thatt natture, nether dyd I thynk, tyll vpon redyng this agayne, my hart could haue bin so vyld as euer to haue conscytted suttch a horyble fact, wheroff I do inffynyttyly repentt me and on my bare knees at my next seing of him wyll aske him humbly pardon.

CHR. BLOUNTE.]

He did not name vnto him any particuler power that wold haue come to him at his landing, but assured him self that his army wold haue bene quickly increased by all sortes of discontented people.

He saieth also that he lyked not to haue had him goe into the citie vppon those small assurances, to which he gaue no creditt, but rather told Sr John Davies it were a much better course if he did first send for his horses into his own court, of which he could haue made presently 120, as he thinketh, and then to haue put Sheriff Smyth to it to haue sent him 500 foote.

This examinat confesseth that, to his remembrance, even at his going into Ireland he confessed to haue practised with Scotland.

He did confesse before his going † that he was assured that many of the Rebells wold be advised by him, but named none in particuler.

He doth also desire that hir Majestie maie be enformed of such other thinges as he hath verbally delivered, and lastly that hir Majestie maye be particulerly informed and remembred of those great services which he did

* On reconsideration Sir Christopher added here the following paragraph.
† That is, into Ireland.

in layeng the waye open to the Erle of Leycester and Mr. Secretary Walsingham for the discovery of all the Queen of Scotts practises, for which hir Majestie was at that tyme (when the Erle of Leycester went into the Lowe Countries) very vnwilling to haue suffred him to haue gone from hir attendance.

He doth now desyre, that seing the fountayn of all this great treason is dryed, that hir Majestie, whose hart he knoweth to be full of mercy, will vouchsafe to haue mercy vppon him, protesting that he can not think, if hir Majestie knewe his own vnspotted deare heart to hir, and what he wold do for hir, she wold not take his lyfe for a million.

CHR. BLOUNTE.

[*Indorsed by Sir Robert Cecil,*]
    Feb. 13, 1600.
    The Examination of Sir Christopher Blunt.

INDEX.

Bacon, Anthony, 40, 88, 90
—— Sir Nicholas, favoured the right of the house of Suffolk to the succession, viii.
Baynham, Sir Edward, 73, 81
Beauchamp, Edward Lord, x.
Berwick, xliii. xlviii. lii.
Bingham, Sir Richard, xlii.
Blackfriars, xlix.
Blunt, Sir Christopher, xx. 102; examination of, 107
Bodley, Mr. 90
Bromley, Sir Henry, 88
Bruce, Edward, abbot of Kinloss, xxix. xxxv. xxxvi. xli. 1, 28, 30, 32, 35, 49, 51, 70; letters of, 38, 45, 51, 78
Burghley, Thomas, second Lord, li. 83
Bushell, Edward, xxvii.

Carey, Sir John, xlviii. xlix. lii.
—— or Carew, Sir George, 83, 92
—— Sir Robert, lii. 49
Carleton, Dudley, letter to, xix.
—— George, extract from letter of, xix.
Cecil, Sir Robert, references and allusions to, *passim;* his character as contrasted with that of Essex, xi.—xvi.; is accused by Essex of favouring the title of the Infanta, xvii. 5, 83; disliked by King James, xxix.; refutes Essex's slander of him, xxxi.—xxxiii.; enters into explanations with James's ambassadors, xxxv.; correspondence with James commenced, xxxvi.; secret well preserved, xxxviii.; his care to keep it close, xxxix. xl.; how the letters were conveyed, xli.; apprises Nicolson of the Queen's illness, xlviii.; forwards proclamation of King James to him, li. 47; Letters of to King James, 3, 12, 17, 20, 27, 33; Northumberland's opinion of him, 67, 75; similar opinion of James, 71
Chaloner, Sir Thomas, 50
Clarence, Duke of, temp. Edward IV. x.
Cobham, Lord, xlix. 39, 73, 82
Coningsby, Sir Thomas, 91
Cuff, Adam, 92
—— Henry, Secretary to Essex, xix. xxv. xxvii. 100, 104, 105, 106; letters of, 81, 85 (2); examination of, 89; will of, 91
—— John, 92

Danvers, Sir Charles, xxii. xxiii. 86, 87, 89, 97, 98; his declaration, 100
Davis, Sir John, xx. 109
Derby, Earl of, x.
Devereux, Lady Dorothy, 91; Lady Frances, 91
Drury House, xvii. xx. 100

Elizabeth, allusions and references to, *passim;* her failing health, v. 46; question of the succession, vi.—xi.; her objection to consider the question, xi.; her last illness, xlviii.—lii. 72; death, liii.
Erskine, Sir Thomas, afterwards Earl of Kellie, xli. 3
Essex, Robert Earl of, allusions and references to, *passim;* his character, xi.; contest for the government with Sir Robert Cecil, xvi.; favours the idea that Cecil was favourable to the Infanta, xvii. xxxi.; his plots, xvii.—xxix. 80—110; his indignation at the disclosures made by his followers, xix.; his own confession and accusations against his friends, xix.; failure of his accusation against Cecil, xxxi.—xxxiii.; his black taffeta bag, 80, 81; instructions prepared by him for Marr, 82, 90

Foulis, David, xxxviii. xli. xliv. 48, 50; letter of, 52
Fullerton, James, afterwards Sir James, xliii. xliv.

Gourden, a Scottish priest, 88
Gray, Master of, xxxviii. 22, 45
Grey, Lord, 95

Hamilton, James, afterwards Lord Clanehoy, xliii. xliv. 43 (?)
Henry VIII. his power of bequeathing the succession, vii.; his will, vii. viii.
Herbert, Lord, 104
—— Secretary, 108
Howard, Lord Henry, xxxviii. 2, 11, 17, 19, 20, 21, 25, 30, 36, 48, 73; letters of or to, 38, 42, 44, 45, 51, 52
Hudson, James, 48
Hunsdon, Lord, 80
Huntingdon, Earl of, x.
Huntley, Marquis of, 29

James VI. of Scotland, allusions and references to, *passim;* his claim to the succession, how derived, viii. ix.; his correspondence with Essex, xviii. xx. —xxix. 86, 90, 96, 102, 103, 108, 109; his instructions to Mar and Bruce, xxx. xxxi.; his ambassadors come to an understanding with Cecil, xxxv.; enters upon a secret correspondence with Cecil, xxxv. xxxvi.; the secret well preserved, xxxviii.; letters published by Lord Hailes, xxxvi.; his agents in Dublin, xliii.; how his mind was influenced by Cecil, xxxviii. xlvi. xlvii.; quietness of his succession, lii.; letters of, to Cecil, 1, 9, 15, 24, 26, 30, 36; to Lord Henry Howard, 42, 44; to Earl of Northumberland, 61, 70, 75; to No. 40 [unknown], 77; to ———, 79

Killigrew, Mr. 91, 92
Kinnaird, xlvii.
Knevet, Mr. xxxii.
Knollys, Sir William, xxxii.

Lee, Henry, 90, 103, 109
Leech, Mr. 92
Lennox, Duke of, 17, 29, 43
Lepton, Mr. xlvii.
Leycester, Robert, Earl of, 116
Littleton, John, xxiv. 87, 90, 97, 98

Mackenzie, 43

Mar, John seventh Earl of, xxv. xxvii. xxviii. xxix. xxxv. xxxvi. 1, 25, 30, 35, 42, 45, 49, 50, 90; instructions for, prepared by Essex, 82, 90
Mary, daughter of Henry VII. doubts as to the validity of her marriage with Charles Brandon, x.
Merton College, Oxford, 92
Montjoy, Lord, xviii. xxi. xxiii. xxiv. xxv. 86, 89, 96, 97, 98, 101, 102, 103, 104, 105, 106, 107
Morrey, Alexander, l.

Neville, Sir Henry, xx. 88, 90, 91, 92, 99
Nicolson, George, xxxviii. xxxix. xliii. xlvi. xlvii. xlix.
Northumberland, Henry Percy Earl of, 47; letter of to King James, 53, 64, 72
Norton, John, bookseller, xxvi. 90, 92
Nottingham, Countess of, xlviii. l. 72
——— Earl of, 80, 90

Oxford, 87, 89, 106

Peyton, Sir John, xxvii. 92, 95; letters of, liii. 80, 81

Raleigh, Sir Walter, 18, 43, 50, 67, 82, 90
Rutland, Earl of, l.

Savage, Sir Arthur, 43
Savile, Henry, 91, 92
Semple, Robert, fourth Lord, 39
Shirley, Sir Anthony, 40, 41
Smyth, Sheriff of London, 109
Southampton, Earl of, xx. xxii. xxiii. xxiv. xxv. 51, 71, 87, 88, 89, 90, 101, 102, 103, 104, 105, 106, 107; letters of, 93, 95; confession of, 96
Spanish Blanks, conspiracy of, xxvi.
Sproxton, Mrs. Dorothy, 92
Stewart, Lady Arabella, lii. 72; her claim to the succession, ix.
Succession to the throne of England on the death of Q. Elizabeth, Acts of Parliament respecting, vi. vii.; legal right in the House of Suffolk, viii; various claims, viii.—xi.; way in which the question was determined by the people, xii.
Suffolk, House of, their right to the succession on death of Elizabeth, viii. x.

Thomas, Valentine, 66
Tyrone, Earl of, xliii. 43, 72, 109

Usher, Archbishop, xliii.

Walsingham, Secretary, 116
Willis, Simon, xl.
Willoughby, Lord, xxvi. 90
Wilson's State of England, xi. n.
Wotton, Sir Henry, xxxix. xl. xli.

Young, Patrick, xli.

Westminster: Printed by J. B. Nichols and Sons, 25, Parliament Street.

www.ingramcontent.com/pod-product-compliance
Lightning Source LLC
Chambersburg PA
CBHW020309170426
43202CB00008B/555